Project Earth Science: Astronomy

Revised 2nd Edition

Table of Contents

Introduction

Activities

Readings

Acknowledgments

Many people contributed to this revision of *Project Earth Science: Astronomy*, as others did to previous editions. This volume began as a collection of Activities and Readings for Project Earth Science (PES), a professional development program for middle school teachers, funded by the National Science Foundation. The Project Earth Science team consisted of middle school teacher leaders, college professors and scientists, and innovators in educational research. The Activities were written and adapted by this team, and have undergone many revisions as a result of using them in the classroom, and feedback provided by other teachers through in-service training.

The principal investigators on the original project were Iris R. Weiss, Diana Montgomery, Paul B. Hounshell, and Paul D. Fullagar. The teacher leaders were Kevin Barnard, Kathy Bobay, Pam Bookout, Betty Dean, Lynanne (Missy) Gabriel, Flo Gullickson, Michele Heath, Cameron Holbrook, Linda Hollingsworth, Geoff Holt, Kim Kelly, Laura Kolb, Karen Kozel, Kim Taylor, Dana White, Tammy Williams, and Lowell Zeigler. Significant contributions were made to the original publication by Kevin Barnard, Missy Gabriel, and Geoff Holt. The original manuscript was reviewed for scientific accuracy by Wayne Christiansen, professor of astronomy at the University of North Carolina at Chapel Hill. We would like to thank all who contributed to the previous editions of *Project Earth Science: Astronomy*. P. Sean Smith was author of the first edition, and part of the PES team.

This edition benefited greatly by the invaluable contributions made by our talented reviewers for their suggestions and feedback, including Gary Sampson, Elaine Lewis, and Paul D. Fullagar. We also thank Adrianna Edwards and Ron Edwards of Focus Strategic Communications Inc., Oakville, Ontario, Canada, for their considerable efforts in preparing this volume for publication. We would also like to thank the rest of the Focus team: Nancy Szostak, designer and formatter; Sarah Waterfield and Carolyn Tripp, illustrators; and Linda Szostak, copyeditor and proofreader.

Project Earth Science: Astronomy, Revised 2nd Edition, is published by NSTA Press. We thank everyone at NSTA who helped with this volume, and especially appreciate the efforts of the publisher, David Beacom. NSTA safety columnist, author, and consultant Ken Roy reviewed the entire manuscript for safety compliance. NSTA Press managing editor Jennifer Horak and project editor Mark Farrell led NSTA's in-house team for the revised second edition.

Introduction

Project Earth Science: Astronomy is part of a four-volume series of Earth science books. The remaining three are *Meteorology, Physical Oceanography*, and *Geology*. Each volume contains a collection of hands-on Activities developed for the middle and junior high school level, and a series of background Readings pertaining to the topic area.

Additions and Changes to Revised 2nd Edition

Activities and Readings have been rewritten to improve clarity and scientific currency, and to suggest additional teaching and learning strategies. The Resources section at the back of this book is almost entirely new. At the beginning of each Activity, there now is a Planner to quickly provide information about that Activity. Material specifically for students, and material specifically for teachers, is more clearly delineated. There are new sections for students within Activities titled What Can I Do? and Fast Fact. Additional new sections included for teachers are How Do We Know This?, Safety Alerts!, Connections, Differentiated Learning, and Assessment.

Within each Activity, there is a section for teachers titled Preconceptions containing a series of questions designed to help draw students into a discussion of the subject. These discussions should reveal students' preconceptions. A preconception is an opinion or view that a student might have prior to studying a particular topic. These opinions may not be accurate because the student does not have the correct information or does not understand that information. Asking students about their preconceptions at the outset of a new instructional topic can provide useful information about what students already know and what misinformation needs to be corrected for them to have a good understanding of the topic.

About *Project Earth Science: Astronomy*

Project Earth Science: Astronomy is based on the concept of the uniqueness of Earth among all the planets in the solar system. Concepts and Activities were chosen that elaborate on this theme. This volume focuses on planetary astronomy and aims to give students a sense of viewing Earth from some point beyond the solar system. By placing Earth in the context of the solar system and viewing it as "just another planet," it is hoped that students will begin to grasp the unique aspects of the planet. Chief among these aspects is that Earth is the only planet in the solar system capable of sustaining life.

This book is divided into three sections: Activities, Readings, and Resources. The Activities in this volume are designed to be hands-on. In collecting and developing these Activities, we tried to use materials that are either readily available in the classroom or inexpensive to purchase.

Each Activity has a student section and a teacher guide. The student section has background information that briefly explains the concepts behind the Activity in non-technical terms. Following this is the procedure for the Activity and a set of questions to guide students as they draw conclusions.

The teacher versions of the Activities, titled Teachers' Guide to Activity X, contain a more detailed version of the background information given to students, and a summary of the important points that students should understand after completing the Activity.

You will find the approximate time to allow for each Activity in the section titled Time Management. The Preparation and Procedure section describes the setup for the Activity and gives sources of materials. Extended Learning gives ideas for challenging students to extend their study of the topic. Use these ideas within the class period allotted for the Activity if time and enthusiasm allow. Interdisciplinary Study includes ideas for relating the concepts in the Activity to other science topics and to other disciplines such as language arts and social studies. The final section of the teachers' guide provides answers to the questions in the student section of the Activity, and discussions on Assessment.

The Activities are followed by a section of Readings for the teacher. One or more of these Readings are referred to in the guide to each Activity. The Readings provide both background information on the concepts underlying the Activities as well as supplementary information to enhance classroom discussions.

A guide to astronomy resources for students and teachers follows on page 163. Though not exhaustive, the guide should give teachers the means to explore this fascinating subject.

Creating Scientific Knowledge

Everyone has wondered if there is life elsewhere in the universe. Could those distant, tiny points of light seen in the night sky have orbiting planets that might also have intelligent life forms? What is it about planet Earth that makes life possible? Do any other planets in our solar system have the same or similar conditions? Do they have water or oxygen? Where are the other planets located in relation to Earth and the Sun?

Ever since the dawn of the space age in 1957, space exploration has advanced our knowledge of the neighboring planets that share our Sun. Robot spacecraft have flown past each of the planets, and orbited Mercury, Venus, Mars, Jupiter, and Saturn. Robotic spacecraft have landed on Venus and Mars. For the first time, we can compare their geological and meteorological conditions with those of Earth. As scientists accumulate this new data, it also reveals how life, as we know it, is unique to Earth.

The space program has given us a snapshot of our own blue and white planet as photographed by journeying spaceships. Imagine what you would see if you could look at Earth from a point above the entire solar system. What would Earth look like, and how big would it be compared to the other planets? Does it spin and revolve like the others? Do the other planets have a moon like Earth's? Is the solar system crowded?

To answer these questions, we must first know where Earth is in relation to all the other planets. The Sun is at the center of the solar system with fast-orbiting Mercury in the first planet position. Venus is next, followed by Earth and Mars as you move out from the Sun. Moving still farther away are the giant planets—Jupiter, Saturn, Uranus, and Neptune.

Only when Earth is placed in the context of the solar system and considered as just another planet do its unique features come to light. NASA's Earth Science Program studies Earth as one global system. This is the perspective NASA has taken in studying every other planet. Now it is turning its attention back to our planet. Some of Earth's unique aspects have already been discovered using this approach. As NASA wrote, "If Earth were much smaller, it could not retain an atmosphere. If it were much closer to or much further from the Sun, the oceans would boil or freeze. If its orbit and axis of rotation did not fluctuate, the cyclical variations in climate that have spurred evolution would not exist."

National Science Teachers Association

Getting Ready for Classroom Instruction

The Activities in this volume are designed to be hands-on. In developing them, we tried to use materials that are either readily available in the classroom or inexpensive to purchase. Note that many of the Activities also could be done as demonstrations.

Each Activity has two sections: a Student section and a Teachers' Guide. Each Student section begins with Background information to explain briefly, in nontechnical terms, what the Activity is about; the Objective states what students will learn. Then there is Vocabulary, which includes important astronomical terms students should know. This is followed by a list of the Materials needed and an estimate of the amount of Time that the Activity will take. Following this introduction is a step-by-step Procedure outline and a set of Questions and Conclusions to facilitate student understanding, encourage constructive thinking, and advance the drawing of scientific conclusions.

Each Student section concludes with additional activities for students in What Can I Do?

The Teachers' Guide contains What Is Happening?, a more thorough version of the background information given to students. The How Do We Know This? section explains techniques or research methods astronomers currently use to generate knowledge related to the Activity. This is followed by possible student Preconceptions, which can be used to initiate classroom discussions. Next comes a summary of What Students Need to Understand. Then Time Management discusses the estimated amount of time the Activity will take. Preparation and Procedure describes the setup for the Activity. Extended Learning challenges students to extend their

study of each topic. Interdisciplinary Study relates the science in each Activity to other disciplines, such as language arts, history, and social sciences. Connections links astronomy to a similar process or concept in geology, meteorology, or physical oceanography. The final portion of each Teachers' Guide includes possibilities for Differentiated Learning, Answers to Student Questions, and suggestions for Assessment.

Although the scientific method often has been presented as a "cookbook" recipe—state the problem, gather information, form a hypothesis, perform experiments, record and analyze data, and state conclusions—students should be made aware that the scientific method provides an approach to understanding the world around us, an approach that is rarely so straightforward. For instance, many factors can influence experimental outcomes, measurement precision, and the reliability of results. Such variables must be taken into consideration throughout the course of an investigation.

As students work through the Activities in this volume, make them aware that experimental outcomes can vary and that repetition of trials is important for developing an accurate picture of concepts they are studying. By repeating experimental procedures, students can learn to distinguish between significant and insignificant variations in outcomes. Regardless of how carefully they conduct an experiment, they can never entirely eliminate error. As a matter of course, students should be encouraged to look for ways to eliminate sources of error. However, they also must be made aware of the inherent variation possible in all experimentation.

Finally, controlling variables is important in maintaining the integrity of an experiment. Misleading results and incorrect conclusions often can be traced to experimentation where important variables were not rigorously controlled. Teachers should encourage students to identify experimental controls and consider the relationships between the variables under study and the factors held under control.

Key Concepts

The Activities in this volume are organized under three broad astronomical concepts:

Key Concept I: Earth's position in the solar system
Key Concept II: Earth's unique properties
Key Concept III: Earth's characteristic phases and seasons

First, students investigate techniques that are used to measure distances and sizes of the magnitude found in the solar system. Using the information gained from these methods, students then place Earth in the solar system in relation to the rest of the planets. Second, students perform activities that stress the uniqueness of Earth. This section focuses on comparisons of Earth to other planets, particularly Venus and Mars. In the third section of the book, students are confronted with two areas of planetary astronomy about which many people have preconceptions: the reason for the phases of the Moon and the explanation of Earth's seasons.

We suggest organizing *Project Earth Science Activities* around these key concepts. To facilitate this approach, the conceptual outline for Astronomy is presented below, with the numbers of the Activities that pertain to each concept.

I. While Earth's position relative to the Sun and other planets is always changing, its distance from the Sun is almost constant. To understand many features of Earth that make it unique and habitable, we need to know where Earth is in relation to the Sun and other planets. Several tools are available to learn where Earth is in the solar system. (Activities 1, 2, 3, 4, and 5)

II. Earth's position in the solar system is responsible for its unique properties. Among these properties is the fact that Earth is the only planet in the solar system that sustains life. (Activities 6, 7, 8, and 9)

III. Many preconceptions exist about Earth and its characteristics. Looking at Earth as "just another planet" can help correct these preconceptions. (Activities 10 and 11)

Project Earth Science: Astronomy and the National Science Education Standards

Effective science teaching within the middle-level age cluster integrates the two broadest groupings of scientific activity identified by the National Science Education Standards: (1) developing skills and abilities necessary to perform scientific inquiry, and (2) developing an understanding of the implications and applications of scientific inquiry. Within the context of these two broad groupings, the Standards identify specific categories of classroom activities that will encourage and enable students to integrate skills and abilities with understanding.

To facilitate this integration, a Standards organizational matrix for *Project Earth Science: Astronomy* appears in the front matter on pages xvi–xvii. The categories listed along the *x*-axis of the matrix, also listed below, correspond to the categories of performing and understanding scientific activity identified as appropriate by the Standards.

Subject and Content. Specifies the topic covered by an Activity.
Scientific Inquiry. Identifies the "process of science" (i.e., scientific reasoning, critical thinking, conducting investigations, formulating hypotheses) employed by an Activity.

xii

Unifying Concepts. Links an Activity's specific subject topic with "the big picture" of scientific ideas (i.e., how data collection techniques inform interpretation and analysis).

Technology. Establishes a connection between the natural and designed worlds.

Personal/Social Perspectives. Locates the specific astronomy topic covered by an Activity within a framework that relates directly to students' lives.

Historical Context. Portrays scientific endeavor as an ongoing human enterprise by linking an Activity's topic with the evolution of its underlying principle.

Safety in the Classroom Practices

The teaching and learning of science today through hands-on, process, and inquiry-based activities make classroom and laboratory experiences effective. Addressing potential safety issues is critical to securing this success. Although total safety cannot be guaranteed, teachers can make science safer by adopting, implementing, and enforcing legal standards and best professional practices in the science classroom and laboratory. Safety in the Classroom Practices includes both basic safety practices and resources specific to the Project Earth Science series. It is designed to help teachers and students become aware of relevant standards and practices that will help make activities safer.

1. When working with glassware, meter sticks, wires, projectiles, or other solid hazards, students use appropriate personal protective equipment (PPE), including safety glasses or goggles, gloves, and aprons.

2. When working with hazardous liquids, indirectly vented chemical splash goggles, gloves, and aprons must be used.

3. Always review Material Safety Data Sheets (MSDSs) with students relative to safety precautions when working with hazardous chemicals.

4. Be careful to wipe up any spilled water on the floor quickly—slip and fall hazard.

5. Be careful when working with the hot plate and hot water—skin can be burned. Have students notify you immediately if someone is splashed with boiling water.

6. Be careful when working with a hot lamp—skin can be burned. Have students notify you immediately if someone is burned.

7. When working with lamps, keep away from water or other liquids—electrical shock hazard.

8. Handle glass thermometers with care so as not to drop or break them—broken glass is a sharp hazard.

9. Know the source of dirt used in an Activity and make sure the source is pesticide- and fungicide-free.

10. Use caution when working with sharp items such as scissors and floral or electrical wires, as they can cut or puncture skin.

11. Wash hands with soap and water upon completing the lab.

12. Use caution when working with pointed objects such as compasses or stakes— impalement hazards.

13. Make sure all trip and fall hazards are removed from the floor prior to darkening the room for an Activity.

14. Keep extension cords off the floor—trip and fall hazards.

15. Make sure that students never look directly at the Sun without appropriate eye protection—major eye hazard.

16. Never eat food or beverage that has been either brought into the lab or used in the lab—potential hazardous chemical contamination.

17. Make sure to abide by school and school district rules on using candy as a reward.

18. When heating liquids, use only heat-resistant glassware (Pyrex- or Kimax-type equipment). Remember that glass labware is never to be placed directly on heating surfaces. Hot containers are potential hazards.

19. When heating liquids on electrical equipment such as hot plates, use ground-fault-protected circuits (GFI).

20. Always remind students of heat and burn hazards when working with heat sources such as hot plates, heating water, and more.

21. Select only markers with low volatile organic compounds (VOC). Some students may be allergic to VOC vapors.

22. Use only asbestos-free vermiculite. Vermiculite containing asbestos will expose students and teacher to this health hazard.

23. Teachers should always model appropriate techniques before requiring students to cut, puncture, or dissect.

For additional safety regulations and best professional practices, go to

NSTA: Safety in the Science Classroom: *www.nsta.org/pdfs/SafetyInTheScience Classroom.pdf*

NSTA Safety Portal: *www.nsta.org/portals/safety.aspx*

Standards Organizational Matrix

Activity	Subject Matter and Content	Scientific Inquiry	Unifying Concepts and Processes
Activity 1 **Measuring the Moon Indirectly**	Indirect measurement of solar system objects	Understanding how to measure large distances	Use of mathematics in astronomy
Activity 2 **Light Year as Distance**	Concept of light year as a unit of distance	Expressing large distances in astronomy	Measurement of large distances
Activity 3 **Solar System Scale**	A scale model of size and distance in the solar system	Determining scale in the solar system	Measurements and models
Activity 4 **The Speed of Light**	Light has a finite speed	Understanding the consequences of light having a finite speed	Effect of finite speed of light on observation of distant objects
Activity 5 **How Far to the Star?**	Parallax (indirect measurement)	Measuring large distances using parallax	Relationship between explanation and evidence
Activity 6 **The Formation of the Solar System**	Solar nebula theory	Modeling accretion	Evidence and models
Activity 7 **Habitable Zone**	Distance and light	Investigating conditions necessary for life on a planet	Interactions among variable conditions within a system
Activity 8 **The Greenhouse Effect**	Nature and behavior of light	Modeling the heat-trapping effect of greenhouse gases	Relationship between explanation and evidence
Activity 9 **Creature Feature**	Compare Earth to Mars and Venus	Comparing possible life conditions on Venus and Mars to Earth	Relationship of life forms to physical environment
Activity 10 **Reasons for the Seasons**	Earth's seasons	Investigating the causes of Earth's seasons	Relationship of Earth's orbit and tilt of axis
Activity 11 **Phases of the Moon**	Moon's phases	Modeling the causes of the Moon's phases	Effects of the Moon's orbit around Earth and solar illumination

National Science Teachers Association

Technology	Personal/Social Perspectives	Historical Context	Key Concept
Technology of measuring devices		Cross-staffs used by ancient peoples for navigation	I
Communicating over large distances			I
		Copernicus developed a scale model of the solar system	I
Finite speed of light and all forms of electromagnetic radiation	The challenges of observing distant objects		I
Technology of measuring devices		Parallax predicted by ancient Greeks	I
		Examining theories of solar system formation	II
Measuring temperatures and distances	Evaluating the conditions for life as we know it		II
	Climate change		II
Technology to measure environmental conditions	Adaptation to extreme environments		II
Use of photocell and multimeter			III
	Evaluating preconceptions about Moon phases		III

Activities at a Glance

Activity	Pages	Subject and Content	Objective	Materials
Activity 1 Measuring the Moon Indirectly	1–9	Indirect measurement of solar system objects	Learn how angular diameter can be used to measure the true diameter of the Moon.	Each group of students will need: paper plate, metric ruler, metric tape measure, index card, scissors, safety glasses or goggles
Activity 2 Light Year as Distance	11–18	Concept of light year as a unit of distance	Develop an understanding of the concept of a unit known as the "light year."	Each group of students will need: watch with second hand or a stopwatch, metric tape measure (30 m or more works best), calculator (helpful but not essential), safety glasses or goggles
Activity 3 Solar System Scale	21–29	A scale model of size and distance in the solar system	Build a scale model of the solar system.	Each group of students will need: trundle wheel, masking tape, eight stakes, eight index cards, sharp pencil, one ball (23.2 cm diameter), drawing compass (optional), solar viewing glasses for each student (optional)
Activity 4 The Speed of Light	31–36	Light has a finite speed	Understand the consequences of light having a finite speed.	Each student will need: a piece of candy or other treat
Activity 5 How Far to the Star?	39–48	Parallax (indirect measurement)	Investigate the factors affecting parallax.	Each group of students will need: construction paper (or manila folder), pencil, metric ruler, chalkboard or large sheets of A1 paper (594 mm x 841 mm), chalk or markers, scissors (if manila folders are used), tape (if manila folders are used), single-hole punch
Activity 6 The Formation of the Solar System	51–58	Solar nebula theory	Observe a model of how the solar system would have originated according to the solar nebula theory.	The class will need: one bag of vermiculite, containers of water placed centrally in the room, 100 mL graduated cylinder, 1,000 mL beaker or comparable container for overhead demonstration Each group of students will need: one stirring rod, one bucket (11 L) for student exercise, basin for collecting used water, 15 mL of vermiculite, indirectly vented chemical splash goggles and apron

Time	Vocabulary	Key Concepts	Margin Features
50 minutes or less	Indirect measurement, Angular diameter, Similar triangles	I	Safety Alert!, Fast Fact, What Can I Do?, Connections
50 minutes or less	Light year	I	Fast Fact, What Can I Do?, Connections
More than 50 minutes but less than 100 minutes	Scale model, Scaling factor	I	Fast Fact, Safety Alert!, What Can I Do?, Connections
Less than 50 minutes	Radio wave, Speed of light, Speed of sound	I	What Can I Do?, Fast Fact, Safety Alert!, Connections
50 minutes	Direct measurement, Indirect measurement, Parallax effect, Baseline	I	Fast Fact, Safety Alert!
Less than 50 minutes	Solar nebula theory, Nebula, Protostar, Protosun	II	Safety Alert!, Fast Fact, Connections

Activity	Pages	Subject and Content	Objective	Materials
Activity 7 Habitable Zone	61–68	Distance and light	Investigate the relationship between distance from a light source and temperature, and apply this relationship to understand why life in the solar system has been found only on Earth.	Each group of students will need: four Celsius thermometers (nonmercury); meter stick, a lamp with a 75-watt bulb, a clamp, and a stand; safety glasses or goggles for each student
Activity 8 The Greenhouse Effect	71–80	Nature and behavior of light	Observe and investigate a model of how light and the atmosphere interact to make Earth suitable for life.	The class will need: one large bag of potting soil, one box of plastic wrap, graph paper for each student Each group of students will need: two large disposable plastic cups, dirt to fill each cup (use commercial potting soil free of pesticide or fungicide), something to prop up thermometers (e.g., a slightly smaller cup or stack of books), one rubber band, two Celsius thermometers (nonmercury), hole punch
Activity 9 Creature Feature	83–90	Compare Earth to Mars and Venus	Consider some of the characteristics of Venus and Mars that make the planets uninhabitable for life as we know it.	Each group of students will need: construction paper (at least three different colors), scissors, glue, aluminum foil, straws, toothpicks, paper cups, transparent tape, floral wire
Activity 10 Reasons for the Seasons	93–103	Earth's seasons	Understand why Earth has seasons.	The class will need: one or two globes mounted so that the axis of rotation is tilted to 23.5° from vertical, a bright light source (lamp with at least a 75-watt bulb and without a shade), (optional) photocell such as a mini panel solar cell, (optional) multimeter or voltmeter
Activity 11 Phases of the Moon	105–116	Moon's phases	Understand the cause of the Moon's phases.	For Part 1, the class will need: one bright lamp (at least 75-watt) without shade, one extension cord, one Ping-Pong ball for each student (an option is polystyrene balls), safety glasses or goggles for each student For Part 2, each pair of students will need: cardboard, 15-cm diameter Styrofoam ball, pencil, black paint suitable for Styrofoam, safety glasses or goggles for each student

Time	Vocabulary	Key Concepts	Margin Features
50 minutes or less	Habitable zone	II	Fast Fact, Safety Alert!, Connections, Resources
50 minutes	Greenhouse effect, Radiant heat, Infrared light	II	Fast Fact, Safety Alert!, What Can I Do?, Connections, Resource
50 minutes		II	Fast Fact, Safety Alert!, What Can I Do?, Connections, Resources
50 minutes	Orbit, Ellipse, Axis, Rotation axis	III	Fast Fact, Safety Alert!, What Can I Do?, Connections, Resources
100 minutes (50 minutes per part)	Phases of the Moon	III	Fast Fact, Safety Alert!, What Can I Do?, Connections, Resources

Activity 1 Planner

Activity 1 Summary

Students use a cross-staff to measure the angular diameter of a paper plate 4 m away. From this, they learn to measure the actual or true diameter of distant objects, such as the Moon, that can only be measured indirectly.

Activity	Subject and Content	Objective	Materials
Measuring the Moon Indirectly	Indirect measurement of solar system objects	Learn how angular diameter can be used to measure the true diameter of the Moon.	Each group of students will need: paper plate, metric ruler, metric tape measure, index card, scissors, safety glasses or goggles

Time	Vocabulary	Key Concept	Margin Features
50 minutes or less	Indirect measurement, Angular diameter, Similar triangles	I: Earth's position in the solar system	Safety Alert!, Fast Fact, What Can I Do?, Connections

Scientific Inquiry	Unifying Concepts and Processes	Technology	Historical Context
Understanding how to measure large distances	Use of mathematics in astronomy	Technology of measuring devices	Cross-staffs used by ancient peoples for navigation

Measuring the Moon Indirectly

Background

It is difficult to measure objects in the solar system because it is so massive. That is why we cannot hold a ruler up to the planets and measure them. There are, however, other ways to measure that do not require going to the object. **Indirect measurements** allow us to measure objects millions of kilometers away without ever leaving Earth. One type of indirect measurement is known as **angular diameter.**

The easiest way to understand angular diameter is to look at an example. If it were possible to stretch two strings from your eye to opposite sides of the Moon, the angle between the strings would be 1/2° if measured with a protractor. The angular diameter of the Moon is 1/2°. What does this mean? (See **Figure 1.1.**)

> **Vocabulary**
>
> **Indirect measurement:** A measurement made by measuring other things. You do not need to be near the object or hold an instrument directly up to it to measure it. Examples of indirect measurement in astronomy include angular diameter and parallax.
>
> **Angular diameter:** The measure of an object's diameter in degrees of an arc, a part of a circle, rather than in linear measurement units (kilometers, for example). This is a type of indirect measurement. Angular diameters are used to calculate diameters of objects in the solar system.

Earth · 1/2° · Moon · (not to scale)

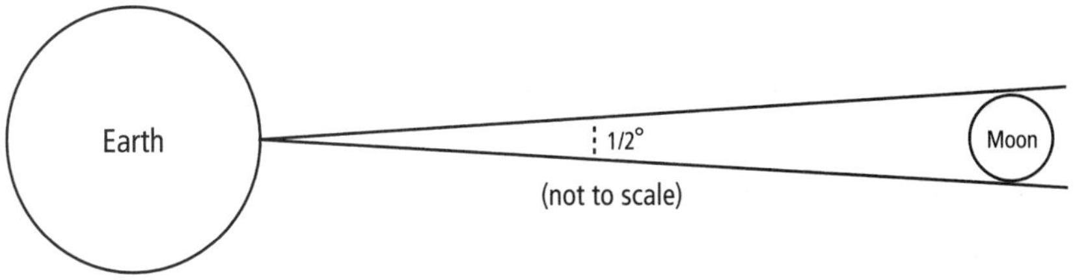

Figure 1.1
The angular diameter of the Moon is ½°.

Objective

Learn how angular diameter can be used to measure the true diameter of the Moon.

Activity 1

Topic: speed of light
Go to: *www.scilinks.org*
Code: PSCA002

Figure 1.2
Index card with
notch and hole

Angular diameters allow us to measure the true size of objects that are very far apart in the solar system. You will learn how that works in this Activity. You will be making a "cross-staff," which was used by ancient peoples for navigation (**Figure 1.2**).

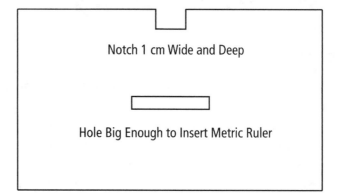

Notch 1 cm Wide and Deep

Hole Big Enough to Insert Metric Ruler

Materials

Each group of students will need

- paper plate
- metric ruler
- metric tape measure
- index card
- scissors
- safety glasses or goggles

Time

50 minutes or less

SAFETY ALERT

Safety glasses or goggles are required for this Activity.

Figure 1.3
Slide the index card along the meter stick until the Moon fits inside the notch.

Procedure

1. Use scissors to cut a notch and hole in the index card, as shown in **Figure 1.2**.

2. Insert the metric ruler through the index card. On the wall, attach the paper plate at eye level or higher.

3. Using the metric tape measure, make sure that your eye is exactly 4 m (400 cm) from the plate. Then, hold the low numbered end of the metric ruler up to your eye. Point it at the paper plate and sight through the notch along the ruler at the plate with one eye, as shown in **Figure 1.3**.

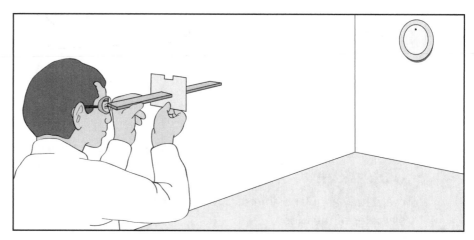

4. Slide the index card along the ruler until the paper plate appears to just fit inside the notch. (This is easier to do if you focus on the notch instead of the plate.) Now the notch and the plate have the same angular diameter.

5. Read the distance to the index card and add 1 cm to this measurement to account for the fact that the ruler was not exactly against your eye. Record this in the data table (**BLM 1.1**).

2

6. Repeat step 5 three more times, recording each measurement in the data table (**BLM 1.1**). Then take the average of the four measurements and record this as well.

7. The following equation uses proportions to find the diameter of the plate. Your teacher will show you how **similar triangles**—triangles with the same angles (congruent angles)— have sides of proportional lengths. Use the equation to calculate the diameter of the plate and record it in the data table (**BLM 1.1**). Even though the notch and plate are different sizes, you moved the index card so that the notch had the same angular diameter as the plate.

$$\frac{\text{Diameter of the plate}}{\text{Width of the notch}} = \frac{\text{distance to the plate}}{\text{average distance to card}}$$

$$\text{Diameter of the plate} = \frac{400 \text{ cm}}{\text{average distance to card}} \times 1 \text{ cm}$$

8. Measure the true diameter of the plate and record it.

Questions and Conclusions

1. Compare the true diameter of the plate with the diameter you calculated. How do the two compare?

2. If the true and calculated diameters are not the same, what could explain the difference?

3. Would this method of determining diameters be helpful in working with the planets in the solar system? Why or why not?

4. The full Moon appears to be bigger when it is on the horizon than when it is high up in the sky. How could you use the angular diameter method shown in this Activity to determine whether this effect is real or an illusion?

5. Write a procedure for using the instrument in this Activity to measure some tall object on the school grounds. You might choose a flagpole, a bus, or the school building. Be sure your procedure is specific enough that others reading it could do the measurement themselves.

Vocabulary

Similar triangles: Two triangles that have equal angles but sides of unequal lengths.

Fast Fact

Aristarchus of Samos published the measurement of Moon's diameter sometime between 310 and 230 BC. He used clever geometry and measurements during lunar eclipses and first and last quarter moons. Archimedes (287–212 BC) reported that Aristarchus measured the diameter to be ½°. Not bad for a measurement made 2,200 years ago!

What Can I Do?

Try this Activity at night when the Moon is full and the sky is clear. You will do everything the same way, except that you will measure the diameter of the Moon instead of a plate. You will probably need a flashlight to illuminate your paper, and someone to help you. You will also need to know the average distance to the Moon: 38,440,100,000 cm. This distance will replace the 4 m measurement in the paper plate Activity.

Data Table

	Distance to Card (cm)	Average Distance to Card (cm)	Diameter of Notch (cm)	Distance to Plate (cm)	Calculated Diameter of Plate (cm)	Measured Diameter of Plate (cm)
Trial 1						
Trial 2						
Trial 3						
Trial 4						

Measuring the Moon Indirectly

What Is Happening?

Objects in the solar system are difficult to measure, primarily because they are so far away. There are, however, indirect ways of measuring these objects—for example, measuring angular diameters. An angular diameter is simply a diameter measured in degrees of an arc rather than centimeters or kilometers. The angular diameter of the Moon is 1/2°, as shown in **Figure 1.4**.

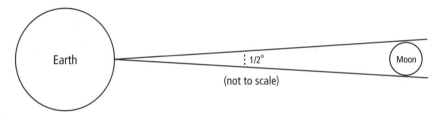

(not to scale)

The angular diameter depends on the distance to the object and the object's diameter. The closer a given object is to the observer, the larger its angular diameter. Also, two objects with different *true* diameters can have the same *angular* diameter. For example, hold a pencil in front of one of your eyes. Use it to just block out your view of a telephone pole, even though the pencil is only a few centimeters long and the pole is several meters high. When you do this, you are adjusting the position of the pencil so that it has the same angular diameter as the telephone pole.

When two objects have the same angular diameter, we can use similar triangles to determine the true diameter of one of the objects as long as the true diameter of the other object is known, and the distances to the objects are known. In similar triangles, the corresponding angles in each are equal even though the corresponding sides may not be, as shown in **Figure 1.5**. Although the corresponding sides are not equal, their ratios are equal. Thus, as long as you know some measurements, you can determine others by setting up the appropriate ratios.

Objective

Learn how angular diameters can be used to measure the true diameter of the Moon.

Key Concept

I: Earth's position in the solar system

Materials

Each group of students will need

- paper plate
- metric ruler
- metric tape measure
- index card
- scissors
- safety glasses or goggles

Time

50 minutes or less

How Do We Know This?

Today, since astronomers cannot use meter sticks to measure the distance to the Moon, they bounce laser light off of reflectors on the Moon and measure how much time it takes for the light to come back.

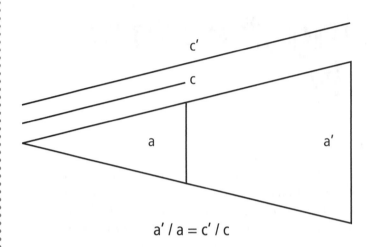

Figure 1.5
Similar triangles

$$a' / a = c' / c$$

Figure 1.6 shows how the principle of similar triangles and angular diameters can be used to determine the true diameter of the Moon. The distance to the card, the distance to the Moon (the paper plate in this Activity), and the width of the notch are all known. This means that the true diameter of the Moon can be calculated using the ratio

$$\frac{\text{diameter of the Moon}}{\text{width of the notch}} = \frac{\text{distance to the Moon}}{\text{distance to the card}}$$

In this Activity, students will learn how to use this method. For the Activity to be more than an exercise in plugging numbers into an equation, you will need to explain to students the properties of angular diameters and similar triangles that make the equation possible, as shown above. These properties are summarized in the next section.

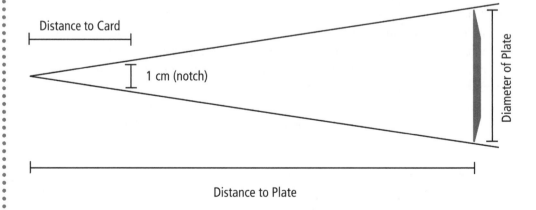

Figure 1.6
Calculating the diameter of the Moon using the principle of similar triangles and angular diameters

Preconceptions

As you begin this Activity, discuss with students the fact that we have known the diameter of the Moon long before *Apollo 8* orbited it. Ask them, "What do you think you know about how astronomers measured the diameter of the Moon and the diameters of other planets in the old days?" You could do this as a whole class discussion or as a Think-Pair-Share to elicit what students already know.

What Students Need to Understand

- Objects that are too far away to measure directly can sometimes be measured using indirect measurements.
- While an object's true diameter is constant, its angular diameter depends on the distance from the object to the viewer; that is, the closer a given object is, the larger its angular diameter.
- Two objects of different size can have the same angular diameter.
- When two objects of different size have the same angular diameter, the principle of similar triangles can be used to determine the size of one of the objects.

Time Management

This Activity will take 50 minutes or less.

Preparation and Procedure

Have all the materials centrally located so that students can obtain them easily. Make sure there is enough space in the room for all students to work at once, either individually or in groups. It is helpful to mark in advance the spaces where groups of students can work.

Consider having the discussion in Preconceptions regarding what they already understand about indirectly measuring the angular diameter.

For additional background information, refer to Reading 1: Angular Diameters.

SAFETY ALERT
Safety glasses or goggles are required for this Activity.

Extended Learning

- Encourage students to carry out the optional activity explained in What Can I Do? They might also want to try the present Activity with other objects besides paper plates, or they may want to try measuring the diameter of the plate again while standing at a different distance.

- Now that spacecraft have reached all the planets, much more accurate planetary data is available. Students might find it interesting to research some of the findings from the recent space missions. For example, they could compare older Earth science or astronomy books with the recent information.
- Have students measure the north/south axis of the Moon during the day. The Moon's third quarter phase is visible in the morning, and the first quarter phase is visible in the afternoon. People often believe that the Moon is visible only at night.

Interdisciplinary Study

- This Activity applies middle school mathematics concepts of congruent angles, proportionality or ratios, scaling, and geometry. Talk with math teachers to make sure you are using the same terminology in the same ways that they do. This will help students recognize the connections between their classes—and see the importance of mathematics.
- Before the advent of small, inexpensive GPS units, geologists, surveyors, and oceanographers used similar triangles to locate themselves on a map. They used a compass and at least two prominent points nearby to "triangulate." The geologist, for example, stood at one corner of a triangle while mountain peaks or radio towers were the two other corners. He or she measured the angles between north and the two points and scaled it down, with similar triangles, to make a map. This was the technique used by geologists who first mapped the West in the 1870s. (Modern geologists use this technique even now, for example, when they are in a steep canyon with poor reception of satellite signals.) Have students learn about the King, Powell, Hayden, and Wheeler Surveys—their purposes, outcomes, and influence on mining, agriculture, railroads, homesteading, and the culture of migration west.
- Have students who are scouts, orienteers, or boaters (who triangulate off buoys) demonstrate how to use a compass.

Differentiated Learning

- Many students struggle with proportions or ratios. To help them use similar triangles, have them draw the measurements on graph paper to a simple scale such as 1 cm = 1 square.
- For students who are adept at or enjoy mathematics, you can challenge them to calculate how much the angular diameter changes because of the eccentricity of Moon's orbit around Earth.

Connections

Meteorologists cannot be everywhere at once. They cannot hold up anemometers in the wind during a storm across an entire region. They can, however, use radar to measure wind and precipitation indirectly. Have students learn how meteorologists use radar to locate dangerous storms and predict where they go.

Answers to Student Questions

1. The comparison depends on students' data. In all likelihood, the two diameters will be close but not the same. Either one may be larger than the other, providing a good opportunity to explore sources of error in measurement.

2. There are many sources of experimental error, including inaccurate measurement (of plate diameter, of index card distance, of notch width, or of distance to plate), not remaining stationary from measurement to measurement, and changing the position of the metric ruler from measurement to measurement.

3. No, you cannot use a cross-staff to measure the angular diameter of planets because they appear too small in the sky—they appear as points of light. Astronomers measure the diameter of a planet by directly measuring the angular size of the planet in a photo taken by a camera attached to a telescope.

4. Calculate the Moon's diameter at moonrise and at "moon noon," when the Moon is highest in the sky. Compare the two. They should be the same.

5. Answers will vary. The important thing is that the procedure students describe is feasible. If time and materials are available, encourage students to try their own procedures. There could even be a class vote to determine the best procedure based on feasibility, clarity, and accuracy of results.

Assessment

• For formal summative assessment, you can grade students' answers to the questions.
• For a more informal assessment, you can ask students to create for a friend in another teacher's class an explanation of how this indirect measurement of angular diameter works.

Activity 2 Summary

Students measure distances by walking heel-to-toe in the unit "student minute." This is to gain an intuitive understanding of light years, a unit in which time represents distance.

Activity	Subject and Content	Objective	Materials
Light Year as Distance	Concept of light year as a unit of distance	Develop an understanding of the concept of a unit known as the "light year."	Each group of students will need: watch with second hand or a stopwatch, metric tape measure (30 m or more works best), calculator (helpful but not essential), safety glasses or goggles

Time	Vocabulary	Key Concept	Margin Features
50 minutes or less	Light year	I: Earth's position in the solar system	Fast Fact, What Can I Do?, Connections

Scientific Inquiry	Unifying Concepts and Processes	Technology
Expressing large distances in astronomy	Measurement of large distances	Communicating over large distances

10

Light Year as Distance

Background

Distances in astronomy are often very difficult to comprehend because they are so large. For example, the distance from the star Sirius to Earth is approximately 81.365 trillion km. This distance is too large for most people to imagine or understand. There are ways, however, to make such large numbers more manageable. For example, it is much easier to understand and work with 15 years than with 5,475 days, even though they both represent the same amount of time. A "year" is just a much larger unit than a "day." The same type of thing can be done with distances using a measurement known as a **light year.**

A light year (abbreviated "ly") is a measurement of distance even though it involves a time unit, the year. A light year is defined as the distance that light will travel in one year. The speed of light is approximately 300,000 km/sec. To calculate how far light travels in one year, first calculate how many seconds there are in a year:

60 sec./min × 60 min/hr × 24 hr/d × 365 d/yr = 31,536,000 sec./yr

So, in one year, light will travel

31,536,000 sec. × 300,000 km/sec.

= 9.461 trillion (9,461,000,000,000) km

= $9.461 × 10^{12}$ km

This is the same as traveling around the world 237 million times.

The light year can make distances easier to understand in the same way that a year makes a large number of days more understandable. Returning to our example above, the distance

Vocabulary

Light year: A unit of measurement equal to the distance light travels in one year (9.461 trillion km or 9,461,000,000,000 km or $9.461 × 10^{12}$ km).

Fast Fact

A trillion is a huge number—it is a thousand billions, a million millions. It is one with 12 zeros attached: 1,000,000,000,000 or 10^{12}. As big as it is, it is a number used annually in the United States to describe our federal budget and our national debt. The U.S. federal budget for Fiscal Year 2010 was $3.55 trillion.

Topic: light year
Go to: *www.scilinks.org*
Code: PSCA011

Objective

Develop an understanding of the concept of a unit known as the "light year."

Activity 2

Materials

Each group of students will need

- watch with second hand or a stopwatch
- metric tape measure (30 m or more works best)
- calculator (helpful but not essential)
- safety glasses or goggles

Time

50 minutes or less

What Can I Do?

To get a sense of how big a trillion is, imagine counting a trillion. See how many coins you can count in a minute, and then calculate how long it would take to count a trillion of them.

to the star Sirius from Earth is approximately 81,365 trillion km. But, this distance is only a little less than 9 ly (8.6 ly), a much more manageable number.

The light year is also important because it tells us about the time lag involved in communicating over the large distances involved in astronomy. If we sent a television or radio signal (both of which travel at the speed of light) to Sirius, it would be almost nine years before it arrived there. In the same way, if Sirius were to somehow stop shining right now, we would not find out about it for almost nine more years, when the last light the star produced finally reached Earth. How old would you be then?

Procedure

1. Find a long distance that you can use either inside or outside the school. This could be a long hallway, a large room such as the cafeteria, a parking lot, or a football field. You will not need a distance longer than a football field.

2. Starting at one end of the space you have chosen, walk heel-to-toe for exactly one minute. Mark where you stop.

3. Use the tape measure to measure how far you walked, rounding to the nearest meter. Record this distance in the data table (**BLM 2.1**).

4. Repeat steps 2 and 3 three more times.

5. Calculate the average of the four measurements and record it in the data table (**BLM 2.1**).

6. The average you calculated is the distance you can walk heel-to-toe in one minute. We will call this distance a "student minute."

Questions and Conclusions

1. Compare the length of your student minute to the calculations made by other students. Are all the student minutes the same? How are they similar?

2. How are student minutes similar to a light year? How are they dissimilar?

3. How many meters are in 3 student minutes? Use the length of your student minute.

4. How many of your student minutes are there in 5,000 m?

5. Listening to the radio one morning at 6:30, you hear that school has been canceled because of damage done in some parts of town by a windstorm. You start to climb back into bed and sleep the day away, but then you remember that your best friend lives in a part of town that was heavily damaged and has no telephone or electricity. Your friend leaves for school every morning at 7:00 and lives 900 m away from you. The only way you can get the news to your friend is to go to your friend's house and deliver the message. If you are only allowed to walk heel-to-toe, can you make it to the house in time based on your own student minute? Explain.

Data Table

	Distance Walked	Average Distance Walked
Trial 1		
Trial 2		
Trial 3		
Trial 4		

Light Year as Distance

What Is Happening?

Distances in astronomy are extremely hard for adults to comprehend, let alone middle or high school students. The units typically used for large measurements on Earth (the kilometer or mile) are too small to be of much help when measuring the distance to stars or other galaxies. For this reason, a unit known as the light year was developed. A light year is defined as the distance that light can travel in one year. Traveling at about 300,000 km/sec., light travels almost 9.461 trillion km in one year.

The light year is a difficult unit for students to understand. The problem lies in the terminology. A time unit—the year—is being used to measure distance. This is familiar to students, however. It is very common to talk about distance in terms of time. Students often talk about how many minutes or hours it takes to get to a friend's house, rather than how many miles it is to get there. A comparison of the time-distance to a friend's house when walking, bicycling, or riding in a car can be a useful illustration of the concept that the time-distance unit depends on the speed of the carrier. Since light is the fastest (and most constant) possible carrier, it is the most useful for establishing the scale of huge astronomical distances.

The light year has another important property that is discussed in more detail in Activity 4: The Speed of Light. The distance in light years that an object is from Earth is the amount of time in years that light from this object would take

Objective

Develop an understanding of the concept of a unit known as the "light year."

Key Concept

I: Earth's position in the solar system

Materials

Each group of students will need

- watch with second hand or a stopwatch
- metric tape measure (30 m or more works best)
- calculator (helpful but not essential)
- safety glasses or goggles

Time

50 minutes or less

How Do We Know This?

How do we know the speed of light? Since light travels incredibly fast, its speed is difficult to measure. Perhaps the easiest method to understand was one of the first direct methods of measurement.

In 1850, French physicist Léon Foucault designed the following method of measuring the speed of light. Light is reflected off a rotating mirror to a stationary mirror located 35 km away. The light reflects off the stationary mirror back to the rotating mirror. But, in the time it takes for the light to go from the rotating mirror to the stationary mirror and back to the rotating mirror again, the rotating mirror would have turned a small amount. By measuring the distance between the two mirrors, the speed at which the mirror was rotating, and how much the angle of the mirror changed, Foucault was able to measure the speed of light to be 298,000 km/sec. This is fairly close to what modern physicists have measured the speed of light to be using laser interferometry—299,792 km/sec.!

to reach Earth. For example, if a star is 12 ly from Earth, light from the star takes 12 years to reach us. Likewise, any light from Earth takes 12 years to reach the star.

This Activity is designed to help students understand the light year by creating for themselves a similar unit that uses time to measure distance. It is important that students understand the nature of the unit, and creating their own unit should aid in this understanding. An important distinction, however, needs to be made between the "student minute" and the light year. The student minute may vary depending on how fast the student walks. The light year does not vary. It is a constant because the speed of light is a constant.

Preconceptions

Ask students to tell you what they know about distances to planets or stars. If their math level is high enough to have learned scientific notation, ask them how they handle very large numbers like the number of stars in a galaxy.

What Students Need to Understand

- Distances in astronomy are too large to work with easily when expressed in units such as kilometers. Using a larger unit makes these numbers easier to manage.
- The light year is a measurement of distance even though it involves a time unit.
- It is very common to express distances in terms of time.
- Light has a finite speed. It takes time for light to travel over any distance.

Time Management

Depending on the availability of watches and tape measures, this Activity should take 50 minutes or less.

Preparation and Procedure

You should determine in advance what area students will use for this Activity. If an outdoor site is chosen, be sure the conditions are such that students can remain outside comfortably for an extended period of time.

Rather than have students measure each time they walk, it may be possible to use a lined football field. Alternatively, you may mark off the distance. This can be done simply with a tape measure and marking paint.

For additional background, see Reading 2: What Is a Light Year? and Reading 3: Hubble Space Telescope.

Extended Learning

- It is helpful for students to gain experience with conversions. One way to accomplish this is to have them convert some distances they are familiar with to their own student minute. They may also find it interesting to convert the distance to some stars, which are recorded in light years, into kilometers.

- Students may gain an appreciation for the relative nearness of the planets by comparing their light time-distance to the distance of some of the stars. Students can find current distances on the internet, or they can use average distances.

Interdisciplinary Study

- The light year is simply a unit that makes vast distances easier to work with, as is explained in the Background section. There are examples of units like this in students' everyday lives. For example, a dozen is just another way of representing 12 of something. It is easier to talk about 10 dozen eggs than 120 of them. An hour is just an easier way of representing 60 minutes. Ask students to think of other units like this in their own experience. In a writing activity, they could invent their own unit, name it, describe it, and explain how it would be used (e.g., what is a "mom minute," as in "Yes, Mom. I'll be there in a minute!").

- Scientific notation is introduced in middle school mathematics, but it is sometimes taught merely as an alternative notation. This Activity offers a chance to provide a context for scientific notation—the very large numbers in astronomy. Scientific notation also offers insights into the confidence a scientist has in a measurement by the number of significant digits reported.

Differentiated Learning

Have mathematically adept students work their calculations in scientific notation. They can also work through the calculations found in the Background section using scientific notation.

Answers to Student Questions

1. No, all the student minutes should not be the same; students may notice that the distances do not vary greatly from one student to another.

2. Student minutes and light years are similar in that they both involve a time unit in a distance measurement. Both involve measuring how far something can travel in a given amount of time. The major dissimilarity is in the size of the respective units. But, also, the light year is a constant because the speed

> **Connections**
>
> The concept of distance in the solar system is sometimes expressed in literature. One example is the poem "A Distant Sun" by Lydia Ferguson. Have students research and read this poem.

> **Connections**
>
> Geologists and oceanographers also use time to measure distances. Petroleum geologists, for example, use the time elapsed between thumping the ground to emit a seismic signal and its reflection back. In their search for oil deposits, this allows them to learn the depths at which rock type changes in a method called "seismic stratigraphy." Have students learn about reflection seismology, LIDAR, and active sonar in order to discover how geologists and oceanographers use time as a proxy for distance.

of light is constant. The student minutes will vary because of the variation in how fast different individuals walk, how large their feet are, and the variation in how fast a person walks at different times.

3. Again, this answer will depend on the student minute. For example, if a student minute is calculated to be 30 m, then the answer is (3 student min.) × (30 m/student min.) = 90 m.

4. This answer will vary depending on the length of each student minute. A student minute of 30 m is reasonable to assume. In this case, the answer would be
5,000 m ÷ 30 m/student min. = 166.7 student min.

5. Assuming 30 m for the student minute, it would take the student 900 m/30 m = 30 student min. to reach the friend's house. Therefore, the student should get there just as the friend is leaving.

Assessment

- For an informal check on student learning, ask students to demonstrate their understanding by creating a definition and explanation of a light year with a Think-Pair-Share.
- For formal summative assessment, you can grade the answers to students' questions.
- You can also ask students to demonstrate that they can convert the distance to our next nearest star, Proxima Centauri, to kilometers. The distance is 4.3 ly.

Activity 3 Planner

Activity 3 Summary

Students calculate scaled distances and planetary diameters to planets in our solar system. They then make a model in a large open space, using their scaled measurements.

Activity	Subject and Content	Objective	Materials
Solar System Scale	A scale model of size and distance in the solar system	Build a scale model of the solar system.	Each group of students will need: trundle wheel, masking tape, eight stakes, eight index cards, sharp pencil, one ball (23.2 cm diameter), drawing compass (optional), solar viewing glasses for each student (optional)

Time	Vocabulary	Key Concept	Margin Features
More than 50 minutes but less than 100 minutes	Scale model, Scaling factor	I: Earth's position in the solar system	Fast Fact, Safety Alert!, What Can I Do?, Connections

Scientific Inquiry	Unifying Concepts and Processes	Historical Context
Determining scale in the solar system	Measurements and models	Copernicus developed a scale model of the solar system

Solar System Scale

Activity

Background

Sizes and distances in the solar system are difficult to visualize. The distance from the Sun to Earth is 150 million km. The diameter of Jupiter is 140,000 km. Both of these measurements are so much larger than anything you ever experience that they are difficult to imagine. But, there is another way of thinking about the solar system that is much simpler. It involves reducing all the sizes by the same amount, for example, dividing all the sizes and distances by two. These new values can be used to make what is known as a **scale model**.

Examples of scale models are all around us. Model railroads are scale models of trains. A globe is a scale model of Earth. The advantage of scale models is that they allow us to determine the distance and size of the true object. All that is needed is the **scaling factor** that was used to make the model. For example, if the wheels of a model car are 10 cm in diameter, and the wheels of a real car are 70 cm, then the scaling factor is 70 ÷ 10 or 7. Now any size in the real car can be determined by looking at the model car. If the door of the model is 20 cm long, then the door of the real car is 20 × 7 or 140 cm long.

Nicolaus Copernicus published his scale model of the solar system out to Saturn in 1543. However, he only had relative distances to the planets. At least one distance measurement was needed to apply his model, and to use his scaling factor to calculate the distances to the other planets. Today, we have very accurate distance measurements to each of the planets. In this Activity, you will apply a scaling factor to these known measurements in order to create a scale model of the solar system.

Vocabulary

Scale model: A model that is proportional in all respects to the object being modeled.

Scaling factor: The factor or proportion that, when multiplied by measurements of a scale model, gives the measurements of the object.

Fast Fact

An astronomical unit is the basic unit of length used to measure distances in the solar system. It is the distance from the center of mass of the Sun to the center of mass of the Earth-Moon system (149,600,000 km).

1 AU = 149,597,870.700 ± 0.003 km ≈ 92,955,807.273 ± 0.002 mi ≈ 8.317 light-minutes ≈ 499 light-seconds
- 1 light-second ≈ 0.002 AU
- 1 gigameter ≈ 0.0067 AU
- 1 light-year ≈ 63,241 AU
- 1 parsec = 648,000/π ≈ 206,264.8 AU

Topic: solar system
Go to: www.scilinks.org
Code: PSCA021

Objective
Build a scale model of the solar system.

Activity 3

Materials

Each group of students will need

- trundle wheel
- masking tape
- eight stakes
- eight index cards
- sharp pencil
- one ball (23.2 cm diameter)
- drawing compass (optional)
- solar viewing glasses for each student (optional)

Time

More than 50 minutes but less than 100 minutes

SAFETY ALERT !

Never look directly at the Sun without appropriate eye protection provided by your teacher—major eye hazard.

What Can I Do?

Many communities have scale models of the solar system at science or nature centers or at public libraries. Find out whether your community has a scale model and visit it. If your community does not have one, you could propose creating one for a facility that many people visit.

Procedure

1. Before starting this Activity, picture in your mind what you think a scale model of the solar system will look like and write a brief description of it. In the scale model you are about to create, the distances to the planets and the sizes of the planets will be 6 billion times smaller than the real solar system. This means that your scaling factor is 6 billion to one, which can be written as 6,000,000,000:1. Discuss your answer with your group.

2. Divide each of the planet diameters and distances to the planets by 6 billion. Record your calculations in the data table (**BLM 3.1**).

3. On one index card, make a small dot to indicate the scaled size of the planet Mercury. Label the dot "Mercury."

4. On another index card, make a dot to represent the scaled size of Venus. Label it "Venus."

5. Continue this process to illustrate the scaled sizes of the rest of the planets.

6. Tape each index card to a stake.

7. In the location designated by your teacher, use the trundle wheel to measure your scaled distances, and create your scale model. Note that the space you have available may not allow you to create your model all the way out to Neptune.

8. At the location of Earth in your model, look back at the Sun. Since this is a scale model, the apparent size of the Sun in your model is the same as how large the Sun appears in the sky from here on the real Earth! If it is a sunny day, and you have solar viewing glasses to allow you to safely look at the Sun, make the comparison for yourself.

9. At your farthest planet from the Sun, look back at the Sun in your model. The apparent size of the Sun in your model is how large the Sun would actually appear from that location in the real solar system!

10. Return back to the Sun's location in your model, picking up the stakes and cards along the way.

Questions and Conclusions

1. Describe what your model looks like. Is this different from what you pictured in your mind in step 1? If so, how is it different?

2. Describe the Sun's appearance as seen from Earth compared to the Sun's appearance as seen from the most distant planet in your model.

3. The nearest star to Earth (excluding the Sun) is Alpha Centauri, 41,343,392,200,000 km away. Where would you place this star in your scale model of the solar system?

4. What are some of the advantages and disadvantages that you see in using a scale model? Be specific and use examples from this Activity.

Object	Distance to Planet (kilometers)	Scaled Distance (meters)	Actual Diameter (kilometers)	Scaled Diameter (millimeters)
Sun (a star)	n.a.		1,391,980	
Mercury	58,000,000		4,880	
Venus	108,000,000		12,100	
Earth	150,000,000		12,800	
Mars	228,000,000		6,800	
Jupiter	778,000,000		142,000	
Saturn	1,430,000,000		120,000	
Uranus	2,870,000,000		51,800	
Neptune	4,500,000,000		49,500	

Solar System Scale

What Is Happening?

Sizes and distances in the solar system are extremely difficult to visualize. The distance from the Sun to Earth is 150 million km. The distance is so great that there is nothing in everyday experience with which to compare it. Working with distances of this magnitude is extremely difficult for students and adults alike.

One way of dealing with these distances is to use scale measurements, a form of indirect measurement. Many models of buildings and cars use scale measurements. To determine true measurements from scale models, you must only know the scaling factor. For instance, if a model car is one-seventh the size of the real car on which it is based, then every measurement on the real car is simply the scaling factor, seven, times the corresponding measurement on the model. If the wheels on the model are 10 cm in diameter, the real wheels are 10 cm × 7, or 70 cm.

In this Activity, students will build a scale model of the solar system using true measurements and a scaling factor. The scaling factor of 6 billion was chosen because of the size of Mercury. If we made the model smaller, it would be difficult for students to make a small enough dot to represent the planet. But, this means that the scaled distance to Neptune is over 700 m! The planets will seem very small, and spaced widely apart. This fact emphasizes one of the important features of the solar system—it is mostly empty space. Students need to be made aware of a shortcoming of this model—it represents the planets as all being aligned on one side of the Sun. In reality, such an arrangement of the planets happens infrequently.

How Do We Know This?

How do we know how far away the planets are?

Today, astronomers use radar (microwaves, a type of radio wave) to bounce a signal off a planet to measure the distance to the planet. They know how fast light travels (including radio light waves), so they measure the time it takes for the signal to travel from Earth to the distant planet, bounce off the surface, and travel back to Earth. Then they calculate the distance. It is very similar to the way bats use echolocation to measure the distance to the bug they are chasing. This type of measurement works for all planets.

Objective
Build a scale model of the solar system.

Key Concept
I: Earth's position in the solar system

Materials
Each group of students will need

- trundle wheel
- masking tape
- eight stakes
- eight index cards
- sharp pencil
- one ball (23.2 cm diameter)
- drawing compass (optional)
- solar viewing glasses for each student (optional)

Time
More than 50 minutes but less than 100 minutes

Fast Fact
The solar system is not empty. There is a constant flow of particles in space such as meteors, asteroids, dust, radiation, plasma, and other fragments. Astrophysicists estimate that less than 10% of the mass of the entire universe consists of the kind of "luminous" matter that we can see.

Preconceptions

Ask students to describe or draw what they imagine our solar system to be like.

What Students Need to Understand

- The solar system is largely empty space.
- A scale model is one way of working with distances that are too large to visualize.
- As long as the scaling factor is known, true measurements can be determined from scale measurements and vice versa.
- The planets are rarely lined up on one side of the Sun.

Time Management

This Activity will probably take more than 50 minutes but less than 100 minutes. One option is to have students do all their calculations and card preparations on the first day, and then have them actually lay out the full model on the second day.

Activity 4: The Speed of Light uses the same solar system scale you have just created. It takes less than a period, so you may want to schedule this at the end of the second day.

Preparation and Procedure

Find a large area for students to lay out their models. It is likely that you will not have an area long enough to lay out the model all the way to Neptune (750 m), but try to find an area where you can lay out the models at least out to Jupiter (130 m). If you are using an outdoor space, it is important to do the outdoor part of the Activity on a day when students will be comfortable outside for a long period of time.

Due to space and time limitations, you may choose to lay out only one of the models together as a class. However, it is still useful for each group to do their own calculations and create their own set of cards.

In step 8, students are asked to look back at the model Sun and possibly compare its apparent size to the apparent size of the real Sun. This can be a powerful experience, and an excellent way to prove the usefulness of a scale model. Purchasing inexpensive solar viewing glasses is well worth the extra effort. However, only use glasses specifically designed for safely viewing the Sun, and inspect the glasses before each use to check for perforations.

For additional background information, refer to Reading 4: Scale Measurements, and Reading 5: The Goldilocks Effect.

Extended Learning

- You can assign groups of students to research individual planets with regard to their important and unique features. Then, once the solar system is laid out, they can conduct a walking tour of the solar system, stopping at each planet to learn about it.
- Now that students have a better appreciation for how much "space" there is between planets and stars, they may be surprised to find that this is not quite the same on galactic scales. Our galaxy, the Milky Way, is a spiral galaxy. The closest spiral galaxy to our own is the Andromeda Galaxy. Both galaxies are roughly the same size, about 100,000 light years in diameter. Using CDs to represent each galaxy, (scale factor is 100,000 ly = 1 CD), have students calculate how far the two CDs should be apart in a scale model of the Milky Way and Andromeda Galaxies. The actual distance between these two galaxies is roughly 2,500,000 light years. The answer is 25 CD-widths, or about 3 m. A good comparison can be made using grains of sand that are approximately 1 mm in diameter. If the Sun is scaled down to the size of a grain of sand, the nearest star (represented by a grain of sand) would be 29 km away. However, if we scale the Milky Way Galaxy down to the size of a grain of sand, the Andromeda Galaxy (another grain of sand) would be only 25 mm away!

Interdisciplinary Study

- Computer models have been particularly useful in meteorology in studying and predicting weather patterns. Many researchers are now trying to create models to study the greenhouse effect and global climate change. They are attempting to use these models to predict the future effects of increased carbon dioxide in the atmosphere. These applications point out some of the advantages and disadvantages of models. Encourage students to investigate the use of models and how these models are different from scale models in other areas of Earth science.
- The solar system has been a source of inspiration for many authors. This is particularly true in science fiction and in poetry. Three examples of poems based on the solar system are "The Planets" by Myra Cohn Livingston, "A Distant Sun" by Lydia Ferguson, and "Jewels" by Myra Cohn Livingston. Ask students to do research to find two more poems based on the solar system.

Differentiated Learning

This activity involves proportional thinking or ratios, something which many students find challenging. Help them by treating a ratio as something we swap at a rate that is not one for one. For example, you swap me one item for six of

Connections

Scale models are used in all aspects of Earth science—meteorology, geology, oceanography, and astronomy. The maps used in these areas can be thought of as scale models. In each case, the purpose of the model is to depict something that is very large in a much smaller size, or something that is very small in a much larger size (like an atom, molecule, or mineral). As with a physical scale model, scientists work with maps and draw inferences from the maps themselves. Have students explore maps at different scales of their own regions. They can measure between two points they know on the map and then use the map scale—the scaling factor—to calculate the real distance. They could do this on traditional paper maps (road maps or topographic maps) or on Google Earth.

mine. That would be a 1:6 scaling factor. You give me one iTunes song, I give you six back. With a 1:600 scaling factor, you give me one, and I give you 600. With a 1:6 billion scaling factor, you swap me one for 6 billion. Similarly, you swap me two for 12 billion of mine. Or, if I give you 18 billion, you give me three. When students are struggling, give them real examples before showing them the mathematical notation.

Answers to Student Questions

1. The inner planets are much closer together than the outer planets. The distance between planets increases as distance from the Sun increases. The model is mostly empty space.

2. The Sun would appear smaller from the most distant planet.

3. Alpha Centauri would be 6,891 km (41,343,392,200,000 km divided by 6 billion) from the Sun in students' models. For comparison, the width (east-west) of the United States is a little over 4,000 km!

4. Students' answers will vary. The scale model allows you to imagine what the actual solar system is like, but it is still difficult to imagine the great distances and sizes.

Assessment

- For informal assessment, ask students to tell you whether their image of the solar system changed, and if so, in what way.

- To check students' answers on **BLM 3.1**, see **Table 3.1** on the next page. For a further check on students' ability to convert distances with a scaling factor, ask them to scale the distance to Ceres, the largest asteroid in the Asteroid Belt (average orbital radius = 4.14×10^8 km or 414 million km).

- For another application, ask students to apply the scaling factor on a road map to determine the actual distance between two familiar points on the map.

Table 3.1: Answers to BLM 3.1 Data Table

Object	Distance to Planet (kilometers)	Scaled Distance (meters)	Actual Diameter (kilometers)	Scaled Diameter (millimeters)
Sun (a star)	n.a.	0	1,391,980	232.0
Mercury	58,000,000	10	4,880	0.8
Venus	108,000,000	18	12,100	2.0
Earth	150,000,000	25	12,800	2.1
Mars	228,000,000	38	6,800	1.1
Jupiter	778,000,000	130	142,000	23.7
Saturn	1,430,000,000	238	120,000	20.0
Uranus	2,870,000,000	478	51,800	8.6
Neptune	4,500,000,000	750	49,500	8.3

Activity 4 Summary

Students carry messages within a scale model of our solar system from Earth to Mercury, Venus, and Mars (perhaps to Jupiter, too) and back, exploring the consequences of light traveling at a finite speed.

Activity	Subject and Content	Objective	Materials
The Speed of Light	Light has a finite speed	Understand the consequences of light having a finite speed.	Each student will need: a piece of candy or other treat

Time	Vocabulary	Key Concept	Margin Features
Less than 50 minutes	Radio wave, Speed of light, Speed of sound	I: Earth's position in the solar system	What Can I Do?, Fast Fact, Safety Alert!, Connections

Scientific Inquiry	Unifying Concepts and Processes	Technology	Personal/Social Perspectives
Understanding the consequences of light having a finite speed	Effect of finite speed of light on observation of distant objects	Finite speed of light and all forms of electromagnetic radiation	The challenges of observing distant objects

The Speed of Light

Background

Everything we see, we see because of light. We see a tree because light reflects off the tree and travels to our eyes. Because light travels so fast (300,000 km/sec.), we have trouble believing that it takes the light any amount of time to travel from the tree to our eyes. For this reason, when we see something happen, we assume that it is happening at that instant. If we go to a baseball game and see a ball being hit, we assume the ball was hit the moment we saw it happen. But, we do not assume the same thing for sound. For example, when we see a bolt of lightning off in the distance, we see the flash of light before we hear the thunder. The light from the lightning reaches us before the sound does because sound travels much more slowly than light (340 m/sec. at 15°C). So, the **speed of light** is much faster than the **speed of sound**.

All forms of light (X-ray, **radio waves**, microwaves, visible light) travel at the same speed—300 thousand km/sec. Light seems to reach us instantly for two reasons: the distances we are familiar with are very short, and light travels a short distance very quickly. When distances become great, the lag grows between something happening and our seeing it happen, just like with the sound of thunder after we see the lightning. For example, the light we are seeing from the Sun actually left the Sun a little more than 8 minutes ago.

Stars other than the Sun are much farther away; therefore, lag time is much greater. Distances to stars are often measured in light years. A light year is the distance that light can travel in one year. If a star is six light years away from Earth, it means that the light leaving the star takes six years to reach us. It also means that the things we are seeing happen on that star actually happened six years ago. In the same way, if there were

Vocabulary

Speed of light: According to Albert Einstein's theory of relativity, the speed of light is constant: 299,800,000 m/sec. (usually rounded to 300,000,000 m/sec. for simplicity). In this book, 300,000 km/sec. is used for comprehension and comparison.

Speed of sound: This varies depending upon the conditions through which sound moves, such as the density and the temperature of the medium. For the purpose of this Activity, the speed of sound at 15°C in air is 340 m/sec.

Radio wave: Like visible light, this is a form of electromagnetic radiation ranging in wavelength from 1 cm to 100 km. Radio waves are low in energy and are used for, among other things, communication with spacecraft. Like all electromagnetic radiation, radio waves travel at the speed of light.

Objective
Understand the consequences of light having a finite speed.

Topic: light
Go to: www.scilinks.org
Code: PSCA031

Activity 4

What Can I Do?

You can use the speed of light and the speed of sound to determine how far away lightning is. The speed of light is 300,000 km/sec. That means that if lightning occurs 1 km away, you will see it essentially instantaneously— 3 millionths of a second.

However, the speed of sound in air is only 0.343 km/sec. at room temperature. The inverse is 2.92 sec./km or 3 sec./km, if you round it for the convenience of counting seconds. Sound takes about 3 sec. to travel 1 km. See a flash of lightning and count seconds. If you count 3 sec. before you hear thunder, the lightning was 1 km away. If you count 6 sec. between flash and thunder, the lightning was 2 km away. In either case, get inside!

people on a planet close to the star looking at us, they would see what happened here six years ago, not what happened today. (Think what you were doing six years ago that they are seeing now!) They will never be able to see anything more recent than six years in our past.

Procedure

This Activity uses the model of the solar system constructed in Activity 3: Solar System Scale. Your teacher will give you the directions for the present Activity.

Questions and Conclusions

1. Did you receive the message from Earth immediately after it was sent? Why or why not?

2. What were the consequences of the message from Earth taking time to reach you?

3. How does what you learned in this Activity apply to sending information to and receiving information from distant spacecraft or rovers by radio waves? Remember that radio waves are a form of light.

4. As all of you walked heel-to-toe, you were modeling light moving through the solar system. What are some strengths and weaknesses of your model?

The Speed of Light

What Is Happening?

In common experience, it is assumed that light travels over any distance instantaneously. This is because the distances we normally encounter are relatively short, and the speed of light is tremendous. However, light does take time to travel, and when the distances become great enough, this becomes significant. An analogy can be made with sound, which travels more slowly than light. If the distance is great enough, there is a lag between seeing an event and hearing the sound that results from it. For example, when we see a bolt of lightning off in the distance, we see the flash of light before we hear the thunder. The light from the lightning reaches us before the sound does because sound travels much more slowly than light.

All forms of light travel at the same speed, 300,000 km/sec. Radio waves, one form of light, are used to communicate with spacecraft. The signals being received from a spacecraft orbiting Saturn take a little more than an hour to reach Earth. The star Sirius (the brightest star as seen from Earth except for the Sun) is almost 9 ly away. This means that the light now reaching Earth from Sirius left the star almost nine years ago. If there are people on a planet orbiting Sirius who are watching Earth, they would now be seeing what happened here nine years ago. All this is because light takes time to travel.

This Activity is designed to help students understand that light does have a finite speed and that this has consequences for us. In order to grasp the meaning of the Activity, it is important for students to understand that light acts as a messenger in the same way that a person can. Both transfer information from one point to another. How quickly the information is transferred depends on the speed of the messenger, whether the messenger is a person or light.

How Do We Know This?

How do scientists measure the speed of light today?

Today, physicists use lasers to measure the speed of light. A laser produces a beam that is made up of only one color (frequency) of light. They use a process called interferometry to measure the wavelength of that light. The speed of light can then be calculated by multiplying the wavelength times the frequency.

Objective

Understand the consequences of light having a finite speed.

Key Concept

I: Earth's position in the solar system

Materials

Each student will need

• a piece of candy or other treat

Time

Less than 50 minutes

Fast Fact

The Sun emits radio waves, providing the first warning of a storm from the Sun. A radio signal is detected within eight minutes after a solar flare leaves the Sun. This gives us a three-day warning to turn off instruments on satellites and warn astronauts on the International Space Station.

Preconceptions

Ask students, "What do you already know about the speed of light?"

- Light travels at the same speed through all media.
- Different colors or wavelengths of light travel at different speeds.

What Students Need to Understand

- Light takes time to travel.
- Distances must be very great in order for the consequences of the speed of light to become apparent.
- A fundamental consequence of the finite speed of light is that we always see a star's past, never its present.
- Another consequence of light's finite speed is that we cannot control a distant spacecraft in real time.

Time Management

This Activity will take less than 50 minutes. It may be possible to do it on the same day as day 2 of Activity 3: Solar System Scale.

Preparation and Procedure

This Activity should be done in conjunction with Activity 3: Solar System Scale, or a similar activity on the solar system. It also assumes that students are familiar with a light year, as described in Activity 2: Light Year as Distance. Assuming some kind of scale model of the solar system has been built (for example, the one in Activity 3: Solar System Scale), there is very little preparation required. Simply prepare the "messenger" cards, and purchase the candy for students. You can save time by dividing students into their planet groups and designating the messengers prior to the Activity.

For additional information, refer to Reading 2: What Is a Light Year? and Reading 3: Hubble Space Telescope.

Instructions

1. Select two volunteers or designate two students to be the "electromagnetic messengers."

2. Divide the class into three or four groups and position one group at each of the following planets in your scale model of the solar system: Mercury, Venus, Mars, and possibly Jupiter. (Depending on how much time you have, you may not be able to wait until the message reaches Jupiter and students there return.) Have students face away from Earth.

3. Tell the class that you will be on Earth sending out radio messages into the solar system via the electromagnetic messengers. Also tell students that when they receive the message, they must read it silently.

4. The electromagnetic messenger will walk heel-to-toe. Students must also walk heel-to-toe when they travel.

5. Since sound cannot travel in outer space, there must be no talking.

6. Send the messenger out into the solar system with a card for each planet that is inhabited. Each card should read, "Mr./ Ms. _____ is on Earth handing out a limited amount of candy to hungry astronauts. Go to Earth if you want some candy. Remember, you must walk heel-to-toe, and NO TALKING!"

7. As students arrive, hand each one a piece of candy inconspicuously and direct their groups to the questions.

Extended Learning

- Encourage students to come up with a more elaborate skit to demonstrate consequences of light having a finite speed. This would be an excellent opportunity for students to work in cooperative learning groups.

- Have students investigate how engineers deal with the fact that they cannot control their distant spacecraft, lander, or rover in real time. Based on their experience with remote control cars and video games, students assume the robots are controlled in the same fashion.

Interdisciplinary Study

- Light is electromagnetic radiation. It includes infrared, visible, ultraviolet, X-rays, and more. All forms of light travel at exactly the same speed. The various forms of light have both harmful and helpful effects. X-rays revolutionized diagnostic medicine. Too much X-ray radiation, however, is harmful. Students can investigate the uses of all the different forms of light and their effects on humans.

- Various forms of light provide valuable information for astronomers about the universe. The idea behind the Hubble Space Telescope was to place a device to gather radiation (ultraviolet, visible, and infrared) above the atmosphere where it could get unobstructed access to these types of light from objects in space. When light travels through the atmosphere, it can be refracted, reflected, or absorbed, making it difficult to get an accurate picture of the light from planets and stars with a ground-based telescope. In orbit around Earth, Hubble receives light that is unaffected by Earth's atmosphere. See Reading 3: Hubble Space Telescope for a more detailed description.

SAFETY ALERT

Make sure that you abide by school and school district rules on using candy as a reward.

Connections

Just as astronomers look back in time, geologists do, too, but in a different way. By studying rocks and mountains, geologists discern the way Earth used to be—where there used to be mountain ranges and volcanoes, shallow seas and continents. As a writing activity that integrates astronomy and geology, use the following scenario:

A huge mirror has been discovered 50 million light years from Earth in space. With your telescope, you can focus on the mirror and see a reflection of Earth. Your telescope is so powerful that you can make out as much detail as a small river on Earth. Write an essay that describes what you would see happening on Earth and when in Earth's past these things would have happened. (This would be 100 million years ago, as light reflected from the Earth had to travel 50 million years to reach the mirror, then another 50 million years to reach the telescope.)

Connections

Light can be modeled as a wave (and also as a particle). Waves have relevance in other areas of Earth science besides astronomy. Some geologists, for instance, study waves of energy that spread out from the site of an earthquake. Oceanographers study ocean waves, and they use sound waves to plumb the depths of ocean basins. Encourage students to compare and contrast these different waves.

- The idea of seeing a star's past brings up the topic of time travel. In a sense, we are going back in time when we observe any star because we see the star's past as though it were the present. Time travel is a popular theme in science fiction. Madeleine L'Engle's *Wrinkle in Time* is an account of traveling through time between the planets. Encourage students to research the theme of time travel in literature.

- The poem "Messages" by Myra Cohn Livingston describes some of the different messages we receive from space. Encourage students to research and investigate the poem.

Differentiated Learning

Be aware that some students might take their creation of a student minute unit, used here and in Activity 2: Light Year as Distance, too literally. While we assume the speed of light to be constant, a student's own pace varies, and will differ from other students' heel-to-toe paces. If students do not bring this up, consider leading a discussion about it.

Answers to Student Questions

1. No. It took time for the messenger to reach each planet. He or she did not get there instantaneously.

2. All students got the message "late." For the farthest students, this meant not getting to Earth before the candy ran out.

3. Any information we send or receive takes time to travel—even at the speed of light. For example, if NASA wants a spacecraft to make a turn at a certain time, the message must actually be sent hours before then so that it will have time to arrive.

4. Answers will vary, but it is important for students to recognize that each student walked at his or her own pace, and probably varied the pace as well. In contrast, we assume the speed of light to be constant on its path from Earth to a planet and back.

Assessment

- For formal assessment, you could grade students' questions.

- For a more informal approach, you could ask students to imagine being an astronaut on Mars or the operator of a Mars rover from Earth. Ask them, "How does the speed of light affect your communication with the other planet?"

Activity 5 Summary

Students conduct two experiments with parallax by viewing a pencil against a backdrop marked with equally spaced lines. In the first experiment, students note the shift in the apparent position of the pencil by viewing it with each eye at various distances. In the second experiment, they discover the effect of changing the length of the baseline.

Activity	Subject and Content	Objective	Materials
How Far to the Star?	Parallax (indirect measurement)	Investigate the factors affecting parallax.	Each group of students will need: construction paper (or manila folder), pencil, metric ruler, chalkboard or large sheets of A1 paper (594 mm × 841 mm), chalk or markers, scissors (if manila folders are used), tape (if manila folders are used), single hole punch

Time	Vocabulary	Key Concept	Margin Features
50 minutes	Direct measurement, Indirect measurement, Parallax effect, Baseline	I: Earth's position in the solar system	Fast Fact, Safety Alert!

Scientific Inquiry	Unifying Concepts and Processes	Technology	Historical Context
Measuring large distances using parallax	Relationship between explanation and evidence	Technology of measuring devices	Parallax predicted by ancient Greeks

How Far to the Star? Activity
The Parallax Effect

Background

The dimensions of objects can be measured in two ways—directly and indirectly. A tape measure is an example of a device used to measure things directly. **Direct measurements** are made by stretching a tape or placing a ruler next to an object to find out how long it is. Direct measurements are usually made on objects that can be handled. When objects are too big or too far away to be handled, **indirect measurements** must be made.

Astronomers use several forms of indirect measurement. Scale measurements and angular measurements are discussed respectively in Activity 3: Solar System Scale and Activity 1: Measuring the Moon Indirectly. Another form uses the parallax effect. This effect is easily demonstrated. Hold up your thumb at arm's length; with one eye closed, line up your thumb with some object in the background (**Figure 5.1**). A tree or a telephone pole will work well. Without moving your thumb, switch eyes. Your thumb appears to have moved relative to the objects in the background of your view. This is the **parallax effect**—the apparent movement of an object when viewed against a stationary background from two different points. The distance between the points is the **baseline**. The two different points in this example were each of your eyes; therefore, the baseline is the distance between your eyes. The fact that we have two eyes allows our brain to take advantage of parallax in judging distances.

The parallax effect is often used by surveyors to measure relatively small distances, for example, when building roads.

Vocabulary

Direct measurement: A measurement made using an instrument touching the object or distance being measured.

Indirect measurement: A measurement made by measuring other things. You do not need to be near the object or hold an instrument directly up to it to measure it. Examples of indirect measurement include angular diameter and parallax.

Parallax effect: Usually referred to as "parallax," it is a phenomenon in which an object appears to change positions against a background when viewed from two different points.

Baseline: The distance between the two points of observation when measuring parallax.

Topic: parallax/angular diameters
Go to: www.scilinks.org
Code: PSCA039

Objective
Investigate the factors affecting parallax.

Activity 5

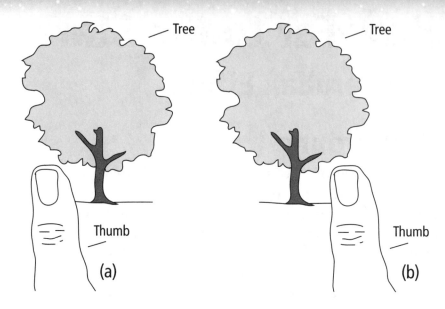

Figure 5.1
This figure shows the parallax effect, the apparent movement of an object from different points. In (a), only the right eye is open, and the tree appears to the right of the thumb. In (b), only the left eye is open, and the tree appears to the left of the thumb.

Materials

Each group of students will need

- construction paper (or manila folder)
- pencil
- metric ruler
- chalkboard or large sheets of A1 paper (594 mm × 841 mm)
- chalk or markers
- scissors (if manila folders are used)
- tape (if manila folders are used)
- single hole punch

Time

50 minutes

Direct measurements could also be used for these distances, but not for distances to objects that are too far away for humans to reach, such as the stars. The parallax effect is one of the few ways we have to measure these cosmic distances from here on Earth.

Procedure
Experiment I

In this part of the Activity, you will determine the effect on parallax of the distance of the object from the observer.

1. Draw a series of equally spaced vertical lines 3 cm apart across the chalkboard (or large sheets of paper), and number them in order as shown in **Figure 5.2**. Twenty of these lines should be enough.

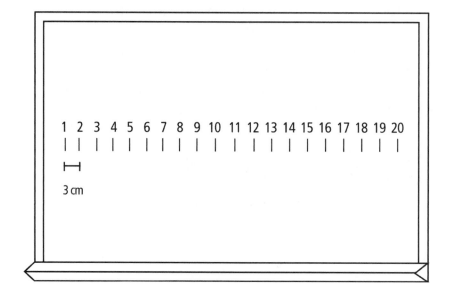

Figure 5.2
An example of equally spaced vertical lines on a chalkboard

2. Have one student stand 2.1 m from the chalkboard and hold up a pencil at arm's length (his or her arm should be parallel to the board). Now, move back away from the chalkboard the distances specified in **BLM 5.1**. Be sure the student holding the pencil stays in the same place.

3. Close your left eye and look at the pencil with your right eye. In **BLM 5.1**, make a mark below the number of the line where you see the pencil.

4. Now, close your right eye and look at the pencil with your left eye, being careful not to move your head. Make another mark for where you see the pencil with your left eye. Repeat steps 3 and 4 for each distance.

The change in position of the object as seen against the lines will be called parallax. For example, if you see the pencil in front of line number 3 with your right eye, but it is in front of line number 9 when looking with your left eye, this is a parallax of 9 – 3 = 6.

A partially completed data table might look like **Table 5.1**, below.

Table 5.1 Data Table Example

Data Table																					
Distance from pencil	1	2	3	4	5	6	7	8	9	10	11	12	13	14	15	16	17	18	19	20	Parallax
1 meter			I				I														6 spaces

Experiment 2

In this part of the Activity, you will determine the effect on parallax of the distance between the two points of observation—the baseline.

1. Find a piece of cardboard or stiff construction paper and punch four holes in it 15 cm apart as shown in **Figure 5.3**. A manila folder torn in half at the fold and taped end to end works well for this.

2. Have someone hold this paper at eye level for you exactly 3 m from the chalkboard. This paper should not move. You will be making all of your observations the same distance from the chalkboard.

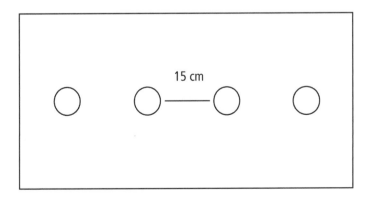

Figure 5.3
An example of holes punched in a piece of stiff material

Activity 5

Fast Fact

Friedrich Bessel, an accountant turned astronomer, was the first to use parallax to measure the distance to a star. In 1838, he published the distance to 61 Cygni.

3. Again, have someone hold the pencil for you in front of the chalkboard with the lines on it, but this time have them hold it 1.8 m from the board.

4. Look at the pencil against the lines through the first hole with one eye and then through the second hole with the same eye. Record the parallax in **BLM 5.2**.

5. Repeat step 4 for the first and third holes and for the first and fourth holes. Record the parallax each time in **BLM 5.2**.

Questions and Conclusions

1. What is the effect on parallax of increased distance to the object being observed?

2. Is it possible that you could move so far away that there would be no parallax?

3. What is the effect of an increased baseline on parallax?

4. What would happen to parallax if you
   (a) increased baseline and decreased distance to the object?
   (b) decreased baseline and increased distance to the object?
   (c) increased baseline and increased distance to the object?
   (d) decreased baseline and decreased distance to the object?

5. What would be challenging about trying to measure the distances to stars using parallax?

6. If you are observing from Earth, what would the maximum baseline be?

7. Hold a sharpened pencil in each hand at arm's length and point them toward each other. With both eyes open, try to touch the points of the pencils together. Now close one eye and try to touch the points again. What happened? Why?

Data Table 1

Distance From Pencil	1 2 3 4 5 6 7 8 9 10 11 12 13 14 15 16 17 18 19 20	Parallax
1 meter		
2 meters		
3 meters		
4 meters		

Data Table 2																				
Baseline	1	2	3	4	5	6	7	8	9	10	11	12	13	14	15	16	17	18	19	20	Parallax
15 cm																				
30 cm																				
45 cm																				

How Far to the Star?
The Parallax Effect

What Is Happening?

Measurements of distance are made either directly or indirectly. When a meter stick or similar instrument is held to an object in order to measure it, a direct measurement is being made. However, when objects are too far away to reach or too big to handle, indirect measurements can be made. One type of indirect measurement of distance takes advantage of the parallax effect.

The parallax effect is a phenomenon in which an object being observed against a stationary background appears to move when observed from two different points. The effect is easily demonstrated by lining up your thumb with some object in the distance, viewing your thumb with one eye, and then viewing it with the other. The thumb appears to move against the background. The brain uses the parallax effect in depth perception. This is possible because humans have two eyes set apart by some distance.

The two main factors that determine the magnitude of the parallax effect are the distance to the object being observed and the distance between the two points of observation, known as the baseline. As distance to the object increases, parallax decreases. For this reason, parallax is helpful in observing the closest stars. As baseline increases, parallax increases. The largest baseline achievable on Earth is the diameter of Earth's orbit around the Sun. To do this, one observation is made, and then a second observation is made six months later. This largest baseline is necessary to measure the distance to the closest stars.

In this Activity, students will investigate the effect of distance to the object and baseline on parallax.

Objective

Investigate the factors affecting parallax.

Key Concept

I: Earth's position in the solar system

Materials

Each group of students will need

- construction paper or manila folder
- pencil
- metric ruler
- chalkboard or large sheets of A1 paper (594 mm × 841 mm)
- chalk or markers
- scissors (if manila folders are used)
- tape (if manila folders are used)
- single hole punch

Time

50 minutes

How Do We Know This?

How do modern astronomers measure the distances to stars?

Astronomers still use parallax to measure the distances to "nearby" stars. Launched in 1989, the European Space Agency's *Hipparcos* (High Precision Parallax Collecting Satellite) mission measured the distances to stars as far away as 1,600 light years. It made many observations of each targeted star, from many positions in its orbit around Earth, and from many positions in Earth's orbit around the Sun. Starting in 2013, Hipparcos' successor, the Gaia mission, hopes to measure the distances to stars that are tens of thousands of light years away.

Preconceptions

Ask students, "What do you think you know about how astronomers measure the distance to planets? To stars?"

What Students Need to Understand

- Distances and sizes in astronomy are often too great to measure directly.
- Parallax is one form of indirect measurement.
- Parallax is the apparent shifting of an object when viewed against a stationary background from two different points.
- Parallax can be used to measure the distance to objects that are too far to measure directly.
- The magnitude of the parallax effect depends on two factors—distance to the object being observed and distance between the two points of observation (baseline).

Time Management

This Activity will take 50 minutes. It could be spread out over two days in a couple of ways. First, if there is only one chalkboard in the room, it will be difficult for all students to participate at once. Alternatively, students could make their 20 lines on large sheets of paper and fasten these to the wall. This could be done on the day before the Activity. Second, the pieces of stiff paper with four holes in them could be constructed ahead of time. If both of these things are done, taking the measurements should consume less than half of a class period.

SAFETY ALERT

Select only markers with low volatile organic compounds (VOC). Some students may be allergic to VOC vapors.

Preparation and Procedure

It is helpful to mark in advance the spaces where students or groups of students can work and to mark lines 1.8 m and 2.1 m from the board. An alternative to having students draw the lines on the board is to draw them on adding machine tape and then attach them to the wall. This can be done beforehand. Have all materials ready and centrally located for distribution. Students will need to work in groups of three in this Activity. Group them before class to save time.

For further information, refer to Reading 3: Hubble Space Telescope and Reading 6: The Parallax Effect.

Extended Learning

- Students may want to determine the actual distance at which they can no longer detect a parallax with just the distance between their eyes as the baseline. They may also like to experiment outdoors with larger distances and baselines. Rather than using lines on the chalkboard, they can use trees or other landmarks as their background.

- Parallax is the fundamental first step for finding distances to stars. To find the distance to planets, parallax has been replaced by methods such as bouncing a radar beam off a planet, and observations from space missions.

- There is another way to demonstrate parallax that involves students in a whole-class activity. It is also a model of the way parallax is used to measure the distance to stars. Take the whole class outside in a large open space—a soccer field, for example. Arrange them as shown in **Figure 5.4**. One student is designated as the near star, which will be observed. About half of the class stands 3 or 4 m behind this student, representing the distant stars. They will be the stationary background against which the near star will be observed. About 15 to 20 m on the other side of the "near star," you stand with the other half of the class arranged in a circle around you. You represent the Sun and the students represent Earth at different positions in its orbit around the Sun. Have students walk around you in a circle and make observations of the near star. Ask them to concentrate on how the near star appears against the background stars from different points in the circle.

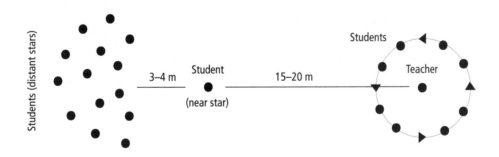

Figure 5.4
The whole class can model the way parallax is used to measure the distance to stars. An example of how students can be arranged is shown in the diagram.

Answers to Student Questions

1. As distance to the object increases, parallax decreases.

2. The obvious and acceptable answer is "yes." The correct answer is actually "no." The parallax is always there. It becomes too small for us to detect it, but it is always there.

3. As baseline increases, parallax increases.

4. (a) Parallax would increase.

   (b) Parallax would decrease.

   (c) The answer depends on how much each factor was changed. The way the two factors are being changed, they offset each other. Therefore, parallax may increase, decrease, or stay the same.

   (d) The same answer as (c).

5. Stars are so far away that their parallax is very small and difficult to detect.

6. Students are likely to figure out that they could maximize the baseline by observing a star from one side of the Earth to the other. Unless you incorporate the activity shown in **Figure 5.4**, students are much less likely to figure out that they could observe a star from opposite sides of the Earth's orbit.

7. Students should not be able to touch the pencil tips together with one eye closed. The reason is that with one eye closed, there is only one point of observation and the brain cannot take advantage of parallax. Therefore, it is much more difficult to tell which pencil is closer and which is farther away. This makes it extremely difficult for students to touch their points.

Assessment

• For an informal assessment, ask students to describe their experience in making the measurements in these experiments. What did they learn? How did they feel about it? Were there any surprises?

• Alternatively, you can ask students what they now know about how astronomers measure the distance to planets and stars.

• For a summative assessment, you could grade answers to questions or have students make a concept map about measurement in astronomy.

Activity 6 Summary

Students create, observe, and analyze a vortex of vermiculite in a bucket of water to model the Solar Nebular Disk Model.

Activity	Subject and Content	Objective	Materials
The Formation of the Solar System	Solar nebula theory	Observe a model of how the solar system would have originated according to the solar nebula theory.	The class will need: one bag of vermiculite, containers of water placed centrally in the room, 100 mL graduated cylinder, 1,000 mL beaker or comparable container for overhead demonstration Each group of students will need: one stirring rod, one bucket (11 L) for student exercise, basin for collecting used water, 15 mL of vermiculite, indirectly vented chemical splash goggles and apron

Time	Vocabulary	Key Concept	Margin Features
Less than 50 minutes	Solar nebula theory, Nebula, Protostar, Protosun	II: Earth's unique properties	Safety Alert!, Fast Fact, Connections

Scientific Inquiry	Unifying Concepts and Processes	Historical Context
Modeling accretion	Evidence and models	Examining theories of solar system formation

The Formation of the Solar System

Background

Over the last four centuries, people have developed many theories to explain the origin and evolution of the solar system. Today, the theory most commonly held by scientists is known as the **solar nebula theory**. The most modern version of the solar nebula theory is called the Solar Nebular Disk Model. It used to be called the nebular hypothesis or accretion theory.

The solar nebula theory explains that a planetary system forms from a huge cloud of gas and dust called a **nebula**. Since each particle has gravity, the particles clump together; those clumps are pulled toward the center of a dense region to form a new star, also called a **protostar** or **protosun**. This process causes the new star to spin, and produces a huge rotating disk of material orbiting around the new star. Astronomers can see this process happening in distant nebulae. These disks look very much like the satellite pictures of hurricanes that you have probably seen on television weather reports. Over millions of years, the material in the disk of our solar nebula accreted, or clumped together, to form the planets presently in the solar system. This theory matches very well with our current understanding of the solar system, including why the planets farther away from the Sun revolve more slowly than the ones closer to the center of the solar system.

In this Activity, you will model what the very early solar system would have looked like, as predicted by the solar nebula theory.

Vocabulary

Solar nebula theory: A theory to explain the formation of our solar system. According to this theory, a cloud of gas and dust collapses under gravity to form a protostar, with material in a disk rotating around the newly formed star. The material eventually clumps together to form planets.

Nebula: A cloud of gas and dust. The nebulae from which stars and planets form are dense clouds of molecular hydrogen, which have been aptly named "giant molecular clouds (GMC)."

Protostar or **Protosun:** An early stage of star formation in which a giant molecular cloud is contracting under its own gravity.

Topic: origin of the solar system

Go to: www.scilinks.org

Code: PSCA051

Objective

Observe a model of how the solar system would have originated according to the solar nebula theory.

Activity 6

Materials

The class will need

- one bag of vermiculite
- containers of water placed centrally in the room
- 100 mL graduated cylinder
- 1,000 mL beaker or comparable container for overhead demonstration

Each group of students will need

- one stirring rod
- one bucket (11 L) for student exercise
- basin for collecting used water
- 15 mL of vermiculite
- indirectly vented chemical splash goggles and apron

Time

Less than 50 minutes

SAFETY ALERT

1. Indirectly vented chemical splash goggles and aprons are required.

2. Be careful to wipe up any spilled water on the floor quickly—slip and fall hazard.

3. Wash hands with soap and water upon completing the lab.

Fast Fact

The first confirmed planet outside our solar system was discovered in 1992. Since then, hundreds of extrasolar planets have been found—in the search for planets and stars with characteristics suitable for sustaining life as we think of it.

Procedure

1. Fill a bucket (or comparable container) three-fourths full with water.

2. Using the graduated cylinder, measure about 15 mL of vermiculite and pour it on top of the water.

3. Stir the mixture vigorously with a stirring rod in a circular motion. When you have a funnel-shaped pattern in the water, stop, remove the stirring rod, and observe.

4. In the space provided on **BLM 6.1**, sketch the pattern of vermiculite that you observe. Label what parts of the pattern might form the inner planets and outer planets of a solar system.

Questions and Conclusions

1. What did you observe happening to the vermiculite once you stopped stirring the water?

2. Describe the pattern of vermiculite on the surface of the water.

3. Did all of the vermiculite spin around in the bucket at the same speed? If not, which parts spun faster and which parts spun more slowly?

4. Why did the vermiculite eventually slow down and stop? Why has the same thing not happened to the solar system?

5. Think about how big your bucket of water and vermiculite is compared to the size of the solar system. Why do you think it took millions of years for the solar system to form? Can you think of reasons other than size?

The Formation of the Solar System

What Is Happening?

Although many theories have been formulated to explain the origin and formation of the solar system, the one most commonly held among astronomers is the solar nebula theory. This theory maintains that the solar system began to form when a rotating interstellar cloud of gas and dust collapsed under its own gravity. This protosun (protostar) was already rotating. As it collapsed, it began to rotate faster and consequently formed a huge flat disk of gas and dust. The gas and dust were not evenly distributed, but were in disconnected parts throughout the disk. The German physicist Baron Carl Friedrich von Weizsäcker (1912–2007) proved theoretically that in such a disk, the outer parts would revolve around the center of the disk more slowly than the inner parts. Later work showed that, over time, the disk would become even more clumped (disconnected); eventually these clumps would become dense enough to fall together under their own gravitation. The clumps then evolved into the planets.

One initial problem with the solar nebula theory was that the Sun has been found to rotate more slowly than the theory would predict. If the disk spins faster as it collapses, the theory predicts that the Sun should spin faster than is actually observed. This problem was solved in the early 1960s with the discovery of the solar wind. This is the stream of charged particles that the Sun is constantly emitting. The Sun's magnetic field is like the spokes of a bicycle wheel carrying streams of charged particles along with it as it spins. This slows

How Do We Know This?

How do we know that there are planets orbiting around other stars?

Today, astronomers use two techniques for detecting exoplanets (planets orbiting other stars). One method, called the spectroscopic method, takes advantage of the fact that orbiting planets tug on their stars, causing them to wobble. They can detect the wobble by studying the star's light. When the star is moving away from us, the light is more red. When the star is moving toward us, the light is more blue.

The other method astronomers are currently using to detect exoplanets is called the transit method. If a planet passes directly in front of its star (called transiting), it will cause a slight drop in a star's brightness. By measuring the time between the drops in brightness, astronomers can determine how long it takes for the planet to orbit around its star.

Objective

Observe a model of how the solar system would have originated according to the solar nebula theory.

Key Concept

II: Earth's unique properties

Materials

The class will need

- one bag of vermiculite
- containers of water placed centrally in the room
- 100 mL graduated cylinder
- 1,000 mL beaker or comparable container for overhead demonstration

Each group of students will need

- one stirring rod
- one bucket (11 L) for student exercise
- basin for collecting used water
- 15 mL of vermiculite
- indirectly vented chemical splash goggles and apron

Time

Less than 50 minutes

down the Sun. This phenomenon, referred to as magnetic braking, is the reason why the planets now have most of the rotational momentum in the solar system rather than the Sun itself.

Today, as hundreds of planets have been found orbiting other stars, and protoplanetary disks are seen around protostars, subtle refinements continue to be made in planetary system formation theories. The most modern version of the solar nebula theory (as of 2010) is called the Solar Nebular Disk Model. This theory was previously called the nebular hypothesis or accretion theory.

This Activity is designed to show students the pattern that is formed when disconnected material clumps together and begins to spin. They will see how the outer parts of the spinning disk revolve relatively slowly, and they may even see some of the material begin to clump together into "planets." Be sure students understand that, unlike the theorized "clumping" of planets due to gravity, the clumps they observe in the vermiculite are not due to gravity, but to cohesion of the vermiculite.

Preconceptions

Probe students about the formation of our solar system system and other planetary systems. You could ask, "What do you understand about how solar systems form? What do you understand about what planets form from?"

What Students Need to Understand

- While many theories concerning the origin of the solar system exist, the one most commonly held by scientists is the solar nebula theory.
- The disk from which the solar system formed was not solid like a discus. It was made of disconnected material as demonstrated in this Activity.
- In a disk such as the one from which the planets formed, the outer parts of the disk revolve more slowly than the inner parts.
- Material rotating in a disk such as the one from which the solar system formed will eventually form clumps due to gravity and the differential speed of revolution. The clumps then become massive enough to attract other material gravitationally, forming a sphere.

Time Management

This Activity will take less than 50 minutes since it does not require data collection and does not take long to set up. For the Activity to take even less time, it may be done as a teacher demonstration by simply placing a beaker containing water and vermiculite on an overhead projector. The image of the rotating disk will be projected on the screen, and you can point out the relevant features.

Preparation and Procedure

Prior to the class, place the buckets, graduated cylinder, stirring rods, and vermiculite in a central location. Vermiculite can be obtained from most garden stores. Have students come and collect their materials, measuring out the vermiculite before returning to their seats.

Extended Learning

- While the solar nebula theory of the origin of the solar system is the predominant one today, this has not always been the case. Other recorded theories date back to the 1600s. Students may be interested in investigating some of these theories. Many introductory astronomy books contain some detail about early and competing theories. Studying these theories could lead easily to a discussion of Kepler's laws.

- One drawback of this experiment is that the disk eventually stops rotating unless stirred periodically. Such stirring, however, disturbs the phenomenon being observed. A solution is to place a magnetic stir bar on the bottom of the beaker or bucket and use the type of hot plate that also stirs. Using heat is not required. Such an arrangement allows students to observe what happens to the vermiculite over an extended period of time.

- Ask students to collect bits of extraterrestrial solar nebula by putting a plastic sheet out in the Sun or a Pyrex® pan out in the rain. They can collect micrometeorites that fall on them with a magnet. Then they can examine them with a magnifying glass or microscope. The bits that look pitted are the micrometeorites. If students need more specific instructions, they can search on the internet for "collecting micrometeorites."

Differentiated Learning

This Activity provides a concrete experience for students who would have difficulty with the abstraction of the Solar Nebular Disk Model. For students who want to analyze their vermiculite vortex further, ask them to compare their model or the theory to hurricanes. How are they similar? How are they different?

Answers to Student Questions

1. Students should see a pattern form in the vermiculite that resembles a satellite photograph of a hurricane. They will also see the disk of material slow down and stop.

2. The vermiculite will probably not be evenly distributed in the disk. Most of it

SAFETY ALERT

1. Indirectly vented chemical splash goggles and aprons are required.

2. Be careful to wipe up any spilled water on the floor quickly—slip and fall hazard.

3. Wash hands with soap and water upon completing the lab.

4. Use only asbestos-free vermiculite. Vermiculite containing asbestos will expose students and teacher to this health hazard.

Connections

Most geologists accept that planetesimals from the solar nebular disk accreted to form Earth. Heat from the accretion—the collision of planetesimals—was sufficient to melt Earth and cause the materials to differentiate essentially by density. You could ask students to learn about the early history of Earth or about current theories of the origin of our Moon.

will be concentrated in the center, becoming less and less dense toward the outer edge of the disk.

3. All the vermiculite should not spin at the same speed. Students should see the inner parts of the disk spinning more rapidly than the outer parts.

4. The vermiculite is floating on water. The water is in contact with the sides and bottom of the bucket creating friction. This friction causes the water, and therefore the disk, to stop spinning. Wind resistance is also a factor, but not nearly as important as the friction between water and bucket. The same thing does not happen in the solar system because there is essentially no friction between the planets and anything else.

5. Responding to this question will require some thought and research on the part of students. Size, thin distribution of matter, and opposing gravitational forces are some factors that could have influenced the formation of the solar system.

Assessment

- To understand what students have learned, you could ask them to "draw and/or describe what you did and what you observed."

- You also could ask students to write in a journal, or ask them in a Think-Pair-Share to revisit the questions in the Preconceptions section, and tell you what they know now that they did not know before.

- You can, of course, grade these or the answers to the questions in the Questions and Conclusions section.

Activity 7 Summary

Students measure temperature over time at different distances from a lamp. They also guess the distance that will give them a target temperature, and then interpolate the distance from their graphed data. Finally, they test their interpolated distance.

Activity	Subject and Content	Objective	Materials
Habitable Zone	Distance and light	Investigate the relationship between distance from a light source and temperature, and apply this relationship to understand why life in the solar system has been found only on Earth.	Each group of students will need: four Celsius thermometers (non-mercury); meter stick; a lamp with a 75-watt bulb, a clamp, and a stand; safety glasses or goggles for each student

Time	Vocabulary	Key Concept	Margin Features
50 minutes or less	Habitable zone	II: Earth's unique properties	Fast Fact, Safety Alert!, Connections, Resources

Scientific Inquiry	Unifying Concepts and Processes	Technology	Personal/Social Perspectives
Investigating conditions necessary for life on a planet	Interactions among variable conditions within a system	Measuring temperatures and distances	Evaluating the conditions for life as we know it

Habitable Zone
How Distance and Temperature Are Related

Background

Earth is the only planet we know of in the solar system that supports life. Although Earth's neighboring planets may be considered to be in the **habitable zone**, neither Venus nor Mars have been found to be habitable. One of them is far too hot and the other is far too cold. Mars has practically no oxygen in the atmosphere, and most of the water is tied up in polar ice caps and permafrost. On Venus, the temperature stays around 460°C. The highest confirmed temperature ever recorded on Earth was 56.7°C in Death Valley, California, on July 10, 1913. If Earth were either closer or farther away, life as we know it never would have evolved.

In this Activity, you will investigate the way distance from a light source affects temperature—one of the many reasons why Earth is "just right" in its ability to support life.

Vocabulary
Habitable zone: A narrow range of distances from a star in which conditions are suitable to sustain life as we know it.

Fast Fact
Although Thomas Edison often is credited with inventing the lightbulb, Frederick de Moleyns was granted the first patent for a lightbulb in England in 1841. Edison's first U.S. patent was not filed until 1878.

Objective
Investigate the relationship between distance from a light source and temperature, and apply this relationship to understand why life in the solar system has been found only on Earth.

SCI LINKS
THE WORLD'S A CLICK AWAY

Topic: the Earth or clement zone
Go to: *www.scilinks.org*
Code: PSCA061

Materials

Each group of students will need

- four Celsius thermometers (nonmercury)
- meter stick
- a lamp with a 75-watt bulb, a clamp, and a stand
- safety glasses or goggles for each student

Time

50 minutes or less

Figure 7.1
Four thermometers arranged along a meter stick at varying distances from a lamp

Procedure

1. In this Activity, you will find where on the meter stick a thermometer should be placed so that the temperature it measures matches a target temperature that your teacher specifies before the experiment begins.

2. After putting on eye protection, place the meter stick on a table. Place the lamp at the end of the meter stick so that light is aimed down along the meter stick as shown in **Figure 7.1**.

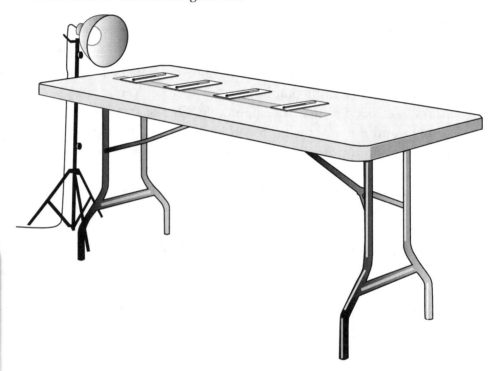

3. Place the thermometers down flat on the meter stick in positions where you think one of them will have a temperature that will match the target temperature. Each thermometer represents a possible distance for Earth from the Sun. Be sure that the bulb of each thermometer is on the meter stick. Record the distance of each thermometer from the end of the meter stick that is next to the lamp in the data table in **BLM 7.1**.

4. Record the starting temperatures for each thermometer in the data table (**BLM 7.1**). Turn on the lamp and record temperatures for each thermometer every 3 min. until no temperature change is seen in any thermometer. Caution: The lamp and reflector will become hot.

5. If none of the final temperatures are the same as the target temperature, graph your results, plotting temperature versus distance. Then try to predict at what distance you should place thermometers when you repeat step 4 so that one of the final temperatures matches the target temperature. If necessary, continue repeating steps 3 and 4 until one of the thermometers reaches the target temperature.

Questions and Conclusions

1. What happened to the temperatures when the light was turned on?

2. How difficult was it to find the position on the meter stick where the final temperature matched the target temperature? Why was this so?

3. How does distance from a source of light (the Sun, for example) affect temperature?

4. How would the temperatures on the gaseous planets (all the planets beyond Mars) compare to the temperatures on Mercury, Venus, Earth, and Mars (the terrestrial planets)?

5. What are some other factors besides distance from the Sun that determine the average temperature of the planet?

6. Based on your observations, do you think we could still live on Earth if the planet moved very much toward or away from the Sun? Why?

7. If Mars or Venus were somehow moved so they were now the same distance from the Sun as Earth, do you think we could live on either of them? Why or why not?

Fast Fact

In the northern hemisphere, the Sun is closer to Earth in the winter than it is in the summer.

Data Table

Trial	Thermometer	Distance to Thermometer	Temperature (°C)					
			Start	3 min.	6 min.	9 min.	12 min.	15 min.
1	1							
	2							
	3							
	4							
2	1							
	2							
	3							
	4							
3	1							
	2							
	3							
	4							

Habitable Zone
How Distance and Temperature Are Related

What Is Happening?

The fact that Earth is the only planet in the solar system that we know supports life is a consequence primarily of its distance from the Sun. If Earth were only 2% of its present distance farther away from the Sun, it would be like Mars— a permanent "ice age" wasteland with a carbon dioxide atmosphere and most of its water tied up in polar ice caps. If Earth were only 5% closer to the Sun, it would be most like Venus, a planet many astronomers have described as a "hellish place." The surface temperature on Venus is about 460°C. Earth's distance from the Sun is just right, and practically no other distance will do. It has only recently been determined that the range of distances from the Sun in which Earth's conditions could have formed is very small compared to the scale of the solar system. Because of this narrow range (or habitable zone), Earth's atmosphere is the only one in the solar system that will allow water to exist in all three states simultaneously—solid, liquid, and gas.

Earth's distance from the Sun has allowed life to flourish here because of one of the properties of light: As the distance from a light source increases, the intensity of the light decreases. That is why in a room with only one light, it

Objective
Investigate the relationship between distance from a light source and temperature, and apply this relationship to understand why life in the solar system has been found only on Earth.

Key Concept
II: Earth's unique properties

Materials
Each group of students will need

- four Celsius thermometers (nonmercury)
- meter stick
- a lamp with a 75-watt bulb, a clamp, and a stand
- safety glasses or goggles for each student

Time
50 minutes or less

How Do We Know This?

How do we know a planet's surface temperature?

In the case of some planets, we have made direct measurements by sending instruments to the surface of Venus and Mars, and into the atmosphere of Jupiter. With other planets, we can calculate a planet's surface temperature without a probe landing there by measuring how much heat the planet is radiating. This is accomplished by measuring the planet's brightness in the infrared part of the spectrum. With some planets, such as Jupiter, Saturn, Uranus, and Neptune, known as "gas giants," astronomers have selected an arbitrary level in the atmosphere to compare to the rocky planets' surface temperatures. Astronomers chose the level in each gas giant's atmosphere where the air pressure would be equal to Earth's air pressure at the surface. So, the "surface temperature" listed for those planets reflects our understanding of each planet's temperature at that depth in the planet's atmosphere.

becomes increasingly difficult to read a book as you move farther away from the source. The intensity of the light decreases with the square of the distance from the source. This means that if you move twice as far away from the source, the intensity of the light will be only one-fourth of what it was. Earth is placed in such a way that it gets just the right intensity of light to allow its unique atmosphere to exist.

This Activity is designed to show students that distance from a light source will affect temperature and that the range of distances in which a specific temperature can exist is relatively small.

Preconceptions

Ask students, "Have you ever seen people or animals use light as a source of heat?" Students might provide interesting examples—heat lamps in bathrooms, chicken brooders, or cats sitting under a lamp, for instance. Then ask, "How does it feel as you get closer to the bulb? How does it feel if you get too close to the bulb?"

What Students Need to Understand

- The intensity of light decreases as you move away from the source.
- As the intensity of light decreases, the temperature resulting from that light will also decrease.
- The temperature on a planet is primarily a consequence of the planet's distance from the Sun. But, there are other factors as well.
- The range of distances from the Sun in which life can exist is very narrow.

Time Management

Including setup and cleanup, this Activity will take 50 minutes or less. Therefore, students could have another task to do between temperature readings. For example, they could be completing an assignment on planetary comparisons that emphasizes the uniqueness of Earth.

Preparation and Procedure

Prior to the class, assemble all the materials in a central location. Make sure that all lamps are working and that none of the thermometers is broken.

Prior to the class period, set up an apparatus and place one thermometer somewhere near the middle of the meter stick. Turn the light on and allow it to remain on until the temperature on the thermometer no longer rises. Let this temperature be the "target temperature" mentioned in the student instructions.

SAFETY ALERT

1. Safety glasses or goggles are required for this Activity.

2. Be careful when working with a hot lamp—skin can be burned. Notify your teacher immediately if someone is burned.

3. Handle glass thermometers with care so as not to drop and/or break them—broken glass is a sharp hazard.

4. When working with lamps, keep away from water or other liquids—electrical shock hazard.

Students will try to determine where on the meter stick to place a thermometer so that its temperature matches the target temperature.

Be sure that thermometers are calibrated. Also, be sure that room temperature does not change much between the time the target temperature is determined and the time this Activity is done. If the room temperature changes too much, the target temperature may actually be below room temperature, making this Activity impossible. For additional information, refer to Reading 8: Global Warming, and Reading 9: The Water Cycle.

Extended Learning

- Some students may want to further investigate the relationship between intensity and distance from a light source. This can be done easily in a room with a single light source and a light meter. It provides an excellent opportunity for students to use graphing skills, plotting distance versus light intensity.

- There are other factors that determine a planet's surface temperature besides light intensity—in particular, the atmosphere. The atmosphere affects temperature through a phenomenon known as the greenhouse effect. In addition to extensive literature on this topic, there are activities that demonstrate it quite well, such as Activity 8: The Greenhouse Effect.

- Astronomers have found hundreds of planets that orbit other stars beyond our solar system. Students may want to investigate discovered planets that are believed to be in the star's habitable zone.

Interdisciplinary Study

Many astronauts have tried to describe what Earth looks like from space and their reactions to the sight. Their accounts provide us with a unique perspective on our planet. The descriptions highlight Earth's beautiful and fragile nature. Some of these accounts can be found at the following websites:
www.spacequotations.com/
www.brainyquote.com/quotes/type/type_astronaut.html
www.solarviews.com/eng/earthsp.htm

- Have students read these accounts and react to them in small group or class discussions. What do these descriptions make students realize about Earth that they did not realize before?

- Have students discuss the uniqueness and fragility of Earth in groups after studying Reading 7: Earth as a System; Reading 9: The Water Cycle; and Reading 11: The Coming Climate Crisis?

Connections

Geologists who study ice ages discuss the effect of changes in the shape of Earth's orbit on the extent of glaciation. The orbit's eccentricity cycles between being more circular and more elliptical on about a 100,000-year scale. This is one component of Milankovitch cycles, named for the engineer and mathematician who first described them. Have students learn about the geologic evidence for these cycles in eccentricity.

Resources

www.spacequotations.com/

www.brainyquote.com/quotes/type/type_astronaut.html

www.solarviews.com/eng/earthsp.htm

Differentiated Learning

Ask students in advanced math classes to graph their data on a graphing calculator. They can then find the best-fit line for their data, determine the sweet spot to match your target temperature, and check their mathematically derived answer experimentally.

Answers to Student Questions

1. All the temperatures rose, but those closer to the light source rose by a greater amount and more rapidly.

2. Answers will depend on students. It may be difficult to find the position since the range of distances from the light source that accompanies the target temperature is small.

3. As distance increases, radiant energy decreases.

4. Since the gaseous planets are farther away, their temperatures should be lower than the temperatures of the inner planets.

5. The atmosphere; the amount of liquid water. For example, Earth's atmosphere helps keep a lot of heat in, and the ocean currents moderate temperatures all over the planet.

6. No. A very small change in the distance from the Sun leads to very drastic changes in conditions on Earth, most notably in temperature.

7. Answers will vary. There is quite a bit of evidence that neither planet would be habitable even if it were in the position of Earth. Evidence from the geologic record suggests that Earth took billions of years to evolve life-sustaining conditions.

Assessment

- While students are making their measurements, monitor them and help them troubleshoot problems by asking open-ended questions (e.g., "Is there another way to do that?" "Describe to me what you've done. Where have you had trouble? What do you think you could do about it?").

- For a summative assessment, you could grade answers to questions. You could also have students demonstrate their graphing and understanding by giving them another set of data and asking them to show you how to find the distance for a target temperature.

Activity 8 Summary

Students measure the temperature in two soil-filled cups sitting in the Sun for about 50 minutes. One cup is uncovered; the other has a clear plastic cover. Students then graph and compare the data from the two cups.

Activity	Subject and Content	Objective	Materials
The Greenhouse Effect	Nature and behavior of light	Observe and investigate a model of how light and the atmosphere interact to make Earth suitable for life.	The class will need: one large bag of potting soil, one box of plastic wrap, graph paper for each student, safety glasses or goggles for each student Each group of students will need: two large disposable plastic cups, dirt to fill each cup (use commercial potting soil free of pesticide or fungicide), something to prop up thermometers (e.g., a sightly smaller cup or stack of books), one rubber band, two Celsius thermometers (nonmercury), hole punch

Time	Vocabulary	Key Concept	Margin Features
50 minutes	Greenhouse effect, Radiant heat, Infrared light	II: Earth's unique properties	Fast Fact, Safety Alert!, What Can I Do?, Connections, Resource

Scientific Inquiry	Unifying Concepts and Processes	Personal/Social Perspectives
Modeling the heat-trapping effect of greenhouse gases	Relationship between explanation and evidence	Climate change

The Greenhouse Effect

Background

Greenhouses are made almost completely of glass for two reasons. First, glass allows the maximum amount of sunlight into the building. Plants need the sunlight for photosynthesis. Second, glass prevents heat produced in the greenhouse from escaping. Clear plastic can also serve these same two functions. When materials like glass and plastic let sunlight, but not heat, pass through them, this is known as the **greenhouse effect**, which is a form of solar heating. How does the greenhouse effect work?

Visible light is only one form of light. **Radiant heat** is **infrared light**, another form. When visible light (sunlight) passes through the glass of a greenhouse, it strikes the objects in the building and its energy is absorbed. These objects begin to heat up. As they heat up, they give off radiant heat—infrared light. While visible light can pass through the glass of the greenhouse, the infrared light cannot. This means that the heat given off by objects in the greenhouse is trapped in the building. Therefore, even on cold, sunny days, the building can stay warm.

Some gases are like the glass of a greenhouse in that they trap heat. Several of these gases, including carbon dioxide (CO_2), water vapor (H_2O), nitrous oxide (N_2O), and methane (CH_4), are present in Earth's atmosphere. The amounts of these gases are increasing daily because of human activities such as driving cars and burning fuel, and because of natural processes such as decomposition in swamps, where methane is released

Vocabulary

Greenhouse effect: A planet's atmospheric layers act like the glass of a greenhouse, permitting sunlight to pass through and strike a planet's surface but reducing the escape of heat (infrared light) radiated from that surface. As a result, the atmosphere warms up.

Radiant heat: Infrared light.

Infrared light: Heat or a form of electromagnetic radiation (light), which has a wavelength ranging from 1 µm to 1 mm. The wavelength of visible light is between 100 and 1,000 times shorter than infrared.

Fast Fact

Cattle are efficient producers of methane, a greenhouse gas. The average cow produces about 81,000 L of methane per year. That's about the amount of methane that seven Toyota Priuses produce. Here's the clincher: In midsummer 2009, there were slightly more than 100 million head of cattle in the United States. That's a lot of methane.

Objective

Observe and investigate a model of how light and the atmosphere interact to make Earth suitable for life.

Activity 8

Materials

The class will need

- one large bag of potting soil
- one box of plastic wrap
- graph paper for each student
- safety glasses or goggles for each student

Each group of students will need

- two large disposable plastic cups
- dirt to fill each cup (use commercial potting soil free of pesticide or fungicide)
- something to prop up thermometers (e.g., a slightly smaller cup or stack of books)
- one rubber band
- two Celsius thermometers (nonmercury)
- hole punch

Time

50 minutes

SAFETY ALERT

1. Safety glasses or goggles are required for this Activity.

2. Handle glass thermometers with care so as not to drop or break them by applying too much force—broken glass is a sharp hazard.

3. Wash hands with soap and water upon completing the lab.

into the atmosphere by decomposing plants and animals. At present, the atmosphere traps only a small part of the heat given off by the surface of Earth. As the amount of carbon dioxide and methane increases, however, Earth may become more like a greenhouse, growing warmer as the atmosphere traps more heat.

This Activity will model how a greenhouse effect can occur.

Procedure

1. Put on eye protection.

2. About 2 cm from the top of each plastic cup, use the hole punch to make a hole big enough for you to insert a thermometer.

3. Fill each cup with dirt until the dirt is about 2.5 cm below the hole you made.

4. Insert a thermometer through each hole so that the bulb is about 2.5 cm above the dirt and centered near the middle of the cup (see **Figure 8.1**). Caution: Do not force the thermometer through the hole. If it will not go, punch a bigger hole.

5. Turn the thermometer so that you can read it.

6. Cover one cup with plastic wrap, and leave the other cup uncovered. Secure the plastic wrap on the cup with a rubber band. The final arrangement should look like **Figure 8.1**.

7. On a sunny day, take the two cups outside at the beginning of the class period, and place them where they will not be disturbed. Stabilize the thermometers so they will not move.

8. Record the initial temperature on each thermometer in **BLM 8.1**.

9. Record temperatures every 5 min. for 30 min. During the first 5 min., write a prediction of what you think will happen to the temperatures of the two cups and give a reason for your prediction. Do this in the space below the data table in **BLM 8.1**.

Figure 8.1
Thermometers measure temperature in the cups, the right one covered with plastic wrap.

10. Make a graph for the temperatures in each cup on a sheet of graph paper (BLM 8.2). Graph the temperatures on the vertical scale and the elapsed time on the horizontal scale. Designate each line as representing either the covered or the uncovered cup.

Questions and Conclusions

1. This Activity is a model of what happens on Earth. What do the dirt and plastic wrap represent in this model?

2. What did you predict would happen?

3. Do your graphs support your prediction?

4. How does what you observed in each cup compare with your prediction? If the two are different, how can you account for this?

5. Describe how you think Earth would be with a thicker atmosphere, and explain your reasoning.

6. What would Earth be like without an atmosphere? Explain your reasoning.

Topic: greenhouse effect/global warming

Go to: *www.scilinks.org*
Code: PSCA073

What Can I Do?

You can be thrifty about your energy use. You can shorten your showers, use only the lights you really need, unplug chargers when they are idle, and turn off a computer at the power strip. Why? Almost half of the electricity Americans use comes from burning coal (49.65% in 2005). When coal burns, it combines with oxygen to make carbon dioxide. When you use less electricity, you reduce the generation of greenhouse gases.

Data Table			
Time (min.)	Temperature of Covered Cup (°C)	Temperature of Uncovered Cup (°C)	Other Observations
0			
5			
10			
15			
20			
25			
30			
35			
Total Difference in Temperature			

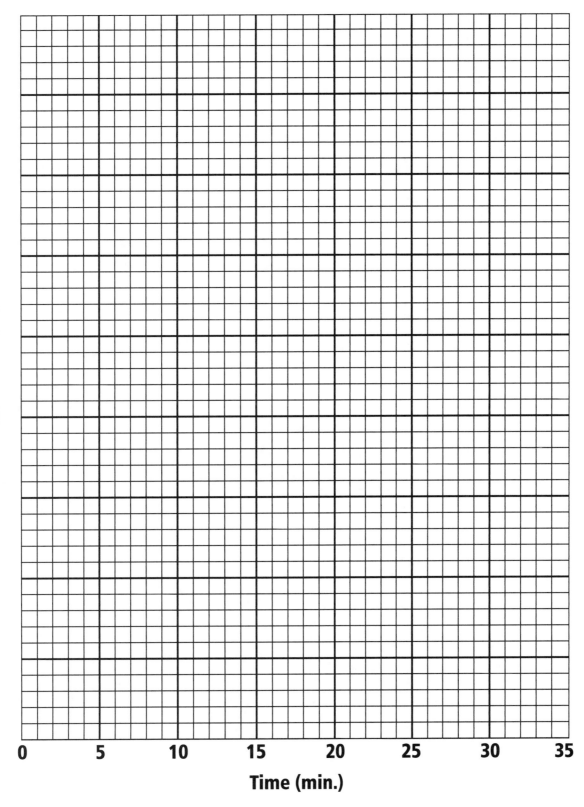

Temperature (°C)

Time (min.)

0   5   10   15   20   25   30   35

The Greenhouse Effect

What Is Happening?

The term *greenhouse effect* refers to the fact that visible light can pass through glass uninhibited, but infrared light (heat) essentially cannot. The term was coined because this effect is most evident in greenhouses. The phenomenon is a consequence of the nature and behavior of light.

Light takes the form of X-rays, gamma rays, ultraviolet light, infrared light, radio waves, and microwaves—not just visible light. As objects in a greenhouse absorb light, they heat up and give off infrared light. While visible light can pass through the glass of the greenhouse, the infrared light cannot and it is reflected back in. So, the heat given off by objects in the greenhouse stays in the greenhouse.

Some gases in Earth's atmosphere, notably carbon dioxide (CO_2), water vapor (H_2O), and methane (CH_4), act like the glass in a greenhouse. Sunlight passes through the atmosphere, strikes the ground, and the ground begins to heat up. The ground then gives off infrared light, which CO_2, H_2O, and CH_4 partially block from escaping the atmosphere. There has always been a natural and beneficial greenhouse effect operating on Earth due primarily to naturally occurring CO_2 and H_2O. Burning fossil fuels, especially since the Industrial Revolution, has increased the concentration of CO_2 in Earth's atmosphere. Estimates for concentration in 1750 were 275 to 285 parts per million (ppm). Measured concentrations in 2005 were 370 ppm. Measurements at the top of Mauna Loa since 1958 show a steady upward trend modulated by seasonal cycles of biological productivity. Global deforestation has compounded the problem by reducing flora that use CO_2 for photosynthesis. As the quantities of these gases grow in the atmosphere, they will prevent more and more of the heat from escaping—which may be causing the temperature of Earth to rise.

For more information on climate change, visit the Intergovernmental Panel on Climate Change (IPCC) at *www.ipcc.ch/*.

Objective
Observe and investigate a model of how light and the atmosphere interact to make Earth suitable for life.

Key Concept
II: Earth's unique properties

Materials
The class will need

- one large bag of potting soil
- one box of plastic wrap
- graph paper for each student
- safety glasses or goggles for each student

Each group of students will need

- two large disposable plastic cups
- dirt to fill each cup (use commercial potting soil free of pesticide or fungicide)
- something to prop up thermometers (e.g., a slightly smaller cup or stack of books)
- one rubber band
- two thermometers (nonmercury)
- hole punch

Time
50 minutes

How Do We Know This?

How do we know which gases are in a planet's atmosphere?
Astronomers study the light coming from a planet to determine which gases are in its atmosphere. This is called spectroscopy. By spreading out the light reflecting off a planet's atmosphere, or the light passing through a planet's atmosphere, astronomers can study its rainbow of colors, or *spectrum*. Each gas absorbs specific colors. So, by looking at which colors are missing, or dim, in a planet's spectrum, astronomers can determine which gases are present. This method is even being used for learning about the atmospheres of planets orbiting other stars!

Preconceptions

Ask students what they know about greenhouses, especially about how they stay warm. Because greenhouses are warmed by infrared radiation, you might also ask them what they know about infrared radiation.

What Students Need to Understand

- Light comes in many forms, not just the visible form that we can see.
- The passage or transmittance of the infrared light (heat) is inhibited by certain things, including glass, CO_2, H_2O, and CH_4.
- CO_2, H_2O, and CH_4 only partially inhibit the passage of heat. Higher concentrations trap more heat.

Time Management

This Activity should take about 50 minutes. You may want to give students assignments to complete between temperature readings. You can save time by having students set up their cups the day before the Activity. It is important to remember that the success of this Activity depends on having a sunny—but not necessarily warm—day.

Preparation and Procedure

Place all the materials in a central location so that students can obtain them easily. Keep track of the weather report and pick a sunny day for the Activity.

Reading 8: Global Warming shows how scientists have come to understand that humans are artificially increasing the amounts of greenhouse gases in the atmosphere, causing the global temperature to rise. Also refer to Reading 10: The Greenhouse Effect, and Reading 11: The Coming Climate Crisis?

Extended Learning

Students may want to see what happens if the cups are left out all day long. Do the temperatures continue to rise? If not, why not? How does this relate to Earth?

This is an excellent place for students to investigate what happens on other planets with regard to the greenhouse effect. Venus and Mars are especially good to research. Students will almost certainly want to know what will happen if the greenhouse effect increases dramatically on Earth. Venus provides a model of what might occur.

Students also can experiment with the effect of the color of the soil on temperature rise. They might want to compare differences between white sand and brown soil on the temperature rise in their greenhouse cups.

SAFETY ALERT

1. Safety glasses or goggles are required for this Activity.

2. Handle glass thermometers with care so as not to drop or break them by applying too much force—broken glass is a sharp hazard.

3. Wash hands with soap and water upon completing the lab.

Finally, students may want to look into current research on the greenhouse effect, and global climate change. This can be a controversial topic in popular media; however, there is a strong consensus among scientists that global surface temperatures have increased in recent decades, and that this is caused mostly by human actions. Have students investigate the human activities that have led to an increase in carbon dioxide in the atmosphere.

Interdisciplinary Study

The oceans play a major role in moderating the amount of carbon dioxide in the atmosphere. The gas dissolves in the ocean and eventually becomes a part of some shells and ocean sediments. Students can investigate research that is being done on the role of the ocean in carbon dioxide regulation.

The greenhouse effect and global climate change are societal as well as environmental problems. Solutions based on environmental concerns alone are incomplete. Industrialized societies depend heavily on burning fossil fuels, the chief source of carbon dioxide in the atmosphere. Solutions to these problems must take into account societal and technological factors as well as environmental ones. What would be the impact on the United States and other industrialized countries of shifting away from fossil fuels? What technology would be required to do this? Are there other possible solutions besides alternative energy sources?

Connections

The greenhouse effect spans all Earth science disciplines: many climatologists, oceanographers, and geologists study the effect of Earth's greenhouse gases through time. Have students learn about the research these scientists do on climate change. What does a geologist or an oceanographer study that is related to climate change (e.g., microfossils and deep ocean currents, respectively)?

Differentiated Learning

Ask students in pre-algebra or algebra classes to confirm their graphing with a graphing calculator, and to extrapolate 10 or 15 min. more than their longest measurement.

Answers to Student Questions

1. The dirt represents the surface of Earth. The plastic wrap represents Earth's atmosphere.

2. Predictions may vary slightly. Pay careful attention to what students predict—it will provide clues for what preconceptions exist in your class and give you guidance about whether to extend this Activity.

3. Students should see a graphical representation of the answer to question 2.

4. The temperature in both cups should have increased, but at different rates. As the dirt in each cup gives off heat, the temperature of each increases. In the covered cup, however, the heat does not escape, so the temperature rises more rapidly.

5. Answers will vary.

Resource

www.ipcc.ch/

6. Answers will vary. Have students applied their experimental results logically to their knowledge about Earth's atmosphere?

Assessment

- While students are doing their experiments, ask them about their procedures and results. Do they believe their results? Do the measurements surprise them or do they seem to make sense? Why? Why not? Would they like to do the experiment differently? If so, how and why?

- For formal summative assessment, you could ask students to graph data or to interpret a graph, you could ask them to write a lab report, or you could grade the answers to the questions.

Activity 9 Summary

Students create Martians and Venusians based on a comparison of the physical, orbital, and atmospheric properties of Mars, Venus, and Earth.

Activity	Subject and Content	Objective	Materials
Creature Feature	Compare Earth to Mars and Venus	Consider some of the characteristics of Venus and Mars that make the planets uninhabitable for life as we know it.	Each group of students will need: construction paper (at least three different colors), scissors, glue, aluminum foil, straws, toothpicks, paper cups, transparent tape, floral wire

Time	Key Concept	Margin Features
50 minutes	II: Earth's unique properties	Fast Fact, Safety Alert!,What Can I Do?, Connections, Resources

Scientific Inquiry	Unifying Concepts and Processes	Technology	Personal/Social Perspectives
Comparing possible life conditions on Venus and Mars to Earth	Relationship of life forms to physical environment	Technology to measure environmental conditions	Adaptation to extreme environments

Creature Feature

Comparing Earth to Mars and Venus

Background

For as long as we have known that there are other planets in the solar system, we have wondered if there might be life on them and if they might support human life. Mars has received most of the attention. Some surface features of Mars that are visible from Earth have, in the past, led some to believe that entire civilizations may have once existed there. In 1976, *Viking I* and *Viking II* landed on Mars and collected soil samples for analysis. The results of these tests did not support the belief that life may have existed on Mars.

Mars and Venus are Earth's closest neighbors. The differences between them are striking. In many ways, Earth can be thought of as the happy medium between the two extremes that Mars and Venus represent. We are aware of many of the forms of both plant and animal life that exist on Earth. Imagine that you were able to create an organism that could survive on Venus or Mars. Would it resemble a plant or animal that you are familiar with? What features would it need for life on these planets? To answer these questions, you will need to become more familiar with the characteristics of Earth's next-door neighbors, Venus and Mars.

Objective

Consider some of the characteristics of Venus and Mars that make the planets uninhabitable for life as we know it.

Fast Fact

The discoverer of Uranus, William Herschel (1738–1822), was also the first to observe that Mars' polar ice caps changed seasonally. In 1783, he drew parallels between Mars and Earth—their orbits, tilted axes of rotation, and changing ice caps. These similarities implied the possibility that Mars was inhabited.

Activity 9

Materials

Each group of students will need

- construction paper (at least three different colors)
- scissors
- glue
- aluminum foil
- straws
- toothpicks
- paper cups
- transparent tape
- floral wire

Time

50 minutes

Fast Fact

There is no significant greenhouse effect on Mars (unlike Venus or the Earth) because Mars only receives about a quarter as much energy from the Sun as does Venus. Also, Venus's atmosphere is very thick—over 90 times the pressure at the surface compared to Earth's. The clouds also trap heat. By contrast, Mars has a very thin atmosphere, with a surface pressure approximately 1% of Earth's.

Topic: Mars
Go to: www.scilinks.org
Code: PSCA084

Procedure

1. Carefully read and study the following brief descriptions of Venus and Mars.

Venus

Venus is the second planet from the Sun, between the orbits of Mercury and Earth. Because it is closer to the Sun than Earth, the sunlight that strikes it is almost twice as intense as that which strikes Earth. The Venusian atmosphere includes a thick cloud cover, and is 96% carbon dioxide. This high concentration of carbon dioxide, coupled with the thick clouds, results in a runaway greenhouse effect (see Activity 8), such that the average surface temperature on Venus is 460°C. The atmosphere is much "thicker" than Earth's, so much so that the air pressure at the surface of the planet is more than 90 times that on Earth. Venus's atmosphere causes most of the sunlight to reflect into space. Only a small portion of the light that does get absorbed by Venus actually makes it to the surface. Consequently, there is a constant eerie, reddish light at the surface of the planet during the day.

The Venusian atmosphere has no oxygen to speak of. It is filled with clouds made of sulfuric acid, a very corrosive substance. The planet rotates slowly compared to Earth. One day on Venus is as long as 117 days on Earth. The surface of Venus is similar to Earth's in composition and density, and Venus is only 5% smaller than Earth. Venus is considered more similar to Earth than any other planet in the solar system, despite important differences in their atmospheres.

Mars

Mars, the next planet beyond Earth, is similar to Earth in several ways as well. The tilt of its rotational axis and its rotational speed are almost identical to that of Earth. Thus, the Martian day is about the same length as Earth's, and Mars has seasons like Earth. The Martian atmosphere is very thin: The air pressure at the surface is 166 times less than that on Earth. Carbon dioxide constitutes 95% of this atmosphere, but unlike Venus, there is no substantial greenhouse effect. Mars's thin atmosphere results in a surface pressure less than 1% of Earth's. Consequently, the planet experiences a wide range of temperatures. The temperature can be as low as –128°C or as high as 37°C during a Martian summer.

At the north and south poles, the temperatures remain cold enough year-round to maintain permanent ice caps made of water ice, with a layer of frozen carbon dioxide (dry ice). The atmospheric pressure on Mars is far too low to allow the existence of liquid water. In addition to the poles, frozen water has been detected beneath the surface at midlatitudes. The thin atmosphere and the lack of a magnetic field make the surface of Mars vulnerable to radiation from the Sun and other stars. The surface of Mars is extensively covered with iron oxide (rust), giving the planet its characteristic red color.

2. In your group, after putting on eye protection and aprons, design and construct a model of some form of life that could survive on Venus. Be sure to include features that are capable of handling the conditions on Venus as described above.

3. Repeat step 2 for Mars.

4. In your group, prepare an explanation of the features of both organisms and designate one or two people in the group to present this to the class.

Questions and Conclusions

1. What features of Venus make it most unlikely that humans or other forms of life from Earth could survive there?

2. What features of Mars make it most unlikely that humans or other forms of life from Earth could survive there?

3. Could the "life form" that you designed for Venus survive on Earth? Why or why not?

4. Could the "life form" that you designed for Mars survive on Earth? Why or why not?

SAFETY ALERT

Wash hands with soap and water upon completing the lab.

What Can I Do?

You can observe both Mars and Venus with just your eyes. Venus will often appear as a bright star-like object above the western horizon at dusk (or the eastern horizon at dawn). With a telescope (or even binoculars), you can make out the phases of Venus, like the phases of the Moon. Mars appears as a reddish dot in the night sky. You can search online for keywords such as "night sky week" for several websites with discussions about what you might observe.

Creature Feature
Comparing Earth to Mars and Venus

What Is Happening?

The purpose of this Activity is to help students understand and appreciate the fact that Earth is the only planet in the solar system known to sustain life. With space exploration came the realization that we may one day be able to travel to other planets in the solar system and that these planets are uninhabitable. Neither the Soviet nor the U.S. missions to Mars and Venus, the planets closest to Earth, have succeeded in finding signs of life past or present on either planet.

In this Activity, students will consider some of the conditions on Venus and Mars that make these planets uninhabitable. (Although our missions to these planets do not indicate life, some scientists believe that Martian meteorites that have been found on Earth seem to have microfossils—see *www.jpl.nasa.gov/snc*. So far, fewer than 20 of these meteorites have been found—and not everyone agrees about what they are, but they have made a big splash in the news.) This Activity may help students appreciate the uniqueness of Earth and learn the importance of being stewards of the planet.

This Activity is well-suited to cooperative learning groups. Consider requiring each group to present their creatures to the entire class and explain them.

Objective

Consider some of the characteristics of Venus and Mars that make the planets uninhabitable for life as we know it.

Key Concept

II: Earth's unique properties

Materials

Each group of students will need

- construction paper (at least three different colors)
- scissors
- glue
- aluminum foil
- straws
- toothpicks
- paper cups
- transparent tape
- floral wire

Time

50 minutes

How Do We Know This?

How do we know what the color of "daylight" would be on another planet?

Scientists and engineers include cameras when they design a spacecraft that will land on another planet. But, they need a way to make sure that the camera is working properly. Sunlight gets filtered and scattered by a planet's atmosphere, so the light that makes it to the surface of another planet will not necessarily be the same colors as those we see here on Earth. So, the engineers include some type of color card on the landing craft, and they can compare what it looks like on that other planet to another card just like it here on Earth. Since we know the gases in a planet's atmosphere, and we know the colors of light that would be absorbed by those gases, the scientists can see if the colors of the card on the lander "make sense."

Preconceptions

Ask students to write or say in a Think-Pair-Share what they think about extraterrestrial life.

What Students Need to Understand

- Earth is the only planet in the solar system that is known to sustain life.
- Through space exploration, we are now aware of specific conditions on Mars and Venus that make life improbable there.

Time Management

This Activity will require at least 50 minutes for groups to construct and present their creatures to the rest of the class. More time will be needed for class and teacher critiques of the creatures.

Preparation and Procedure

Encourage students to use only materials that can be recycled. Be sure to have at least the materials listed on hand, but try to have even more. The more materials students have to work with, the more creative their creatures will be. You may want to prepare in advance a rating scheme so that classes can vote on the best creature for Mars and Venus. If students know the criteria, they might focus better on the conditions on Mars and Venus. You might want to display creatures for all to see. One suggestion is to hang them from the ceiling. For further information, refer to Reading 9: The Water Cycle, and Reading 11: The Coming Climate Crisis?

Extended Learning

Earth's conditions and its life forms are interrelated—each impacts the other. For instance, geologists have evidence that as plants developed, they increased the amount of oxygen in the atmosphere. This made conditions more hospitable for other forms of life.

- We know that human activity is altering the composition of the atmosphere. As an extension to this Activity, have students consider how their creatures might change the conditions on Venus and Mars by their very existence.
- Encourage students to investigate what changes would be necessary to make Mars habitable. Some scientists have suggested that if all the carbon

dioxide frozen in the Martian polar ice caps were in the atmosphere, there might be a sufficient greenhouse effect to make the existence of liquid water possible.

Interdisciplinary Study

- This Activity fits best at the end of the astronomy unit since the descriptions of Mars and Venus, particularly seasons and the greenhouse effect, integrate concepts from the entire unit.
- Alternatively, the Activity could be used in the study of life science once students understand the relevant concepts from astronomy. As students' understanding of life science grows, so will their understanding of the severity of the conditions for life on Mars and Venus. Used in this way, the Activity could serve as a pre- and postassessment to reveal students' increased understanding of the connections between astronomy and life science. As students learn more, their creature's design might change.

Differentiated Learning

- Ask inquisitive students to investigate current efforts to search for life on Mars and the research on origins of life on Earth, which includes the possibility of extraterrestrial "seeds."
- Students can learn about Mars and Venus from Windows to the Universe at *www.windows2universe.org/*, where they can choose beginner, intermediate, and advanced reading levels. The material on this site is also available in Spanish.
- Google Earth also makes Mars approachable for visual learners. Download and install Google Earth at no cost and use the pull-down menu with the icon of Saturn on the menu bar above the window. Search for Google Earth at *www.google.com/earth/index.html*.

Answers to Student Questions

1. Lack of liquid water, lack of oxygen in the atmosphere, high surface temperature, and high atmospheric pressure, among others.

2. Lack of liquid water, lack of oxygen in the atmosphere, low surface temperature, low atmospheric pressure, global dust storms, radiation, among others.

3. Answers will depend on students' models.

4. Answers will depend on students' models.

Connections

Astronomers or planetary geologists who study Mars for signs of life often look for evidence of water. They use the work of geologists on Earth who study things like stream channels, soil patterns, and minerals with water as part of their chemical structure. Have students learn about the techniques used by NASA's Mars Exploration Rovers to explore Mars, especially for signs of water. They could also zoom in on Mars in Google Earth (see Differentiated Learning) to look for features associated with water.

Resources

www.jpl.nasa.gov/snc

www.windows2universe.org/

Assessment

- This Activity lends itself to the power of peer review. Ask students to examine all the creatures, and then discuss what features make sense scientifically, what is whimsical or attractive, what construction techniques worked best, and what makes an effective presentation. Consider allowing students to recreate their creatures after this discussion, given what they have learned.

- For formal assessment, you can grade questions and use a rubric for evaluating creatures.

Activity 10 Planner

Activity 10 Summary

Students use a globe and lamp to model Earth's orbit. From this concrete model, they see and understand that the cause of Earth's seasons is the tilt of its rotational axis.

Activity	Subject and Content	Objective	Materials
Reasons for the Seasons	Earth's seasons	Understand why Earth has seasons.	The class will need: one or two globes mounted so that the axis of rotation is tilted to 23.5° from vertical, a bright light source (lamp with at least a 75-watt bulb and without a shade), (optional) photocell such as a mini panel solar cell, (optional) multimeter or voltmeter

Time	Vocabulary	Key Concept	Margin Features
50 minutes	Orbit, Ellipse, Axis, Rotation axis	III: Earth's characteristic phases and seasons	Fast Fact, Safety Alert!, What Can I Do?, Connections, Resources

Scientific Inquiry	Unifying Concepts and Processes	Technology
Investigating the causes of Earth's seasons	Relationship of Earth's orbit and tilt of axis	Use of photocell and multimeter

Reasons for the Seasons

Background

Many drawings of Earth's **orbit** around the Sun look like **Figure 10.1**. These are meant to give you a view of a nearly circular orbit seen from the side. Rather than a circle, the shape of the orbit in **Figure 10.1** is an **ellipse**. Often, however, people mistakenly think that such drawings show Earth's true orbit.

> **Vocabulary**
>
> **Orbit:** The path followed by one body revolving about another body.
>
> **Ellipse:** The oval shape formed by cutting through a cone.

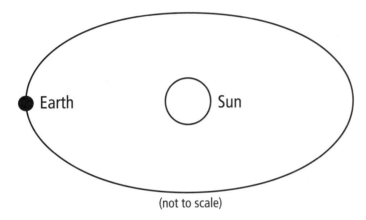

(not to scale)

Figure 10.1
Earth's orbit around the Sun is not the extreme ellipse shown here.

While it is true that Earth does have a slightly elliptical orbit, it is not nearly as extreme as that illustrated in **Figure 10.1**. That picture makes it look like Earth is much closer to the Sun at some times and much farther away at others. Actually, Earth's orbit looks much more like a circle than an ellipse. **Figure 10.2** is a much more accurate representation of Earth's orbit around the Sun.

Topic: reasons for the seasons
Go to: www.scilinks.org
Code: PSCA093

> **Objective**
> Understand why Earth has seasons.

Activity 10

Fast Fact

Although Earth's spin is steady over our lifetimes, over 41,000 years it tips from 22.1° and 24.5° and back. The axis also wobbles like a top in a cycle that lasts 26,000 years.

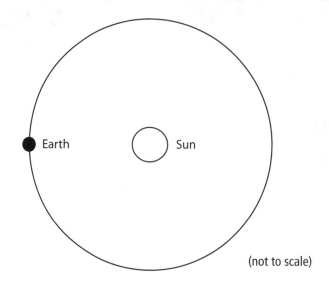

(not to scale)

Figure 10.2
Earth's circular orbit around the Sun

Vocabulary

Axis: A straight line about which a figure or body is symmetrical.

Rotation axis: A straight line around which a body spins.

Many people think that the reason Earth has seasons is because its orbit looks like **Figure 10.1**. They think that when Earth is closest to the Sun, summer occurs, and when it is farthest from the Sun, we have winter. If distance from the Sun determined the seasons, then it should be summer in the southern hemisphere (Argentina, for example) when it is summer in the northern hemisphere (the United States or England), but this is not what happens. When it is summer in the northern hemisphere, it is winter in the southern hemisphere.

The reason Earth has seasons is because of the angle at which it rotates (spins) as it revolves (orbits) around the Sun. If you spin a ball on your finger, it rotates around an **axis** that is straight up and down, but Earth's **rotation axis** is tilted (as shown in **Figure 10.3**), and this tilt causes the seasons. With a model, you will see how the tilt causes the seasons.

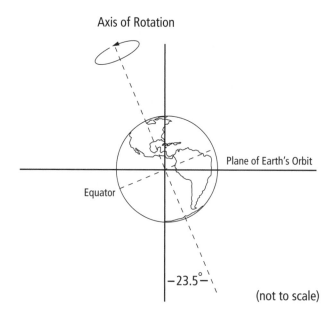

(not to scale)

Figure 10.3
Tilt of Earth's axis

94

Procedure

1. Arrange the lamp and globe(s) as shown in **Figure 10.4**. If you are using two globes, be sure that each is the same distance from the lamp. A minimum distance of 1.5 m from the bulb will work best.

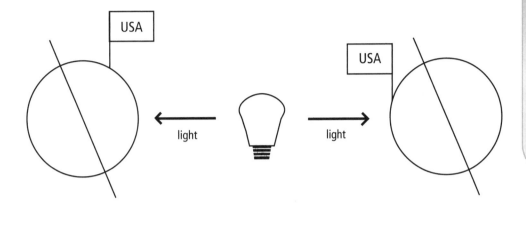

Position 1   Position 2

2. Put on eye protection and darken the room.

3. Make and record observations about the intensity of light on the different parts of the globe that are facing the light.

4. Take one globe and walk it through an orbit around the Sun counter-clockwise as seen from above. Make sure that you maintain the tilt of the axis and keep it oriented in the same direction. At each position, you may want to spin the globe so that the difference from day and night can be observed. For the United States, noon would occur when the United States is facing directly toward the Sun, and midnight occurs when the United States is facing directly away from the Sun. Earth's rotation is counter-clockwise as seen from above the North Pole.

5. Make and record observations about the brightness of light on the United States at noon in Position 1 compared to noon in Position 2.

Questions and Conclusions

1. How did the brightness of light on the United States compare between Positions 1 and 2?

2. How can you account for the differences in the brightness of light?

3. How did the brightness of light on the United States change when you walked the globe around the Sun?

4. At what points in the orbit do you think each of the seasons would occur?

5. When it is summer in the United States, where might it be winter?

Materials

The class will need

- one or two globes mounted so that the axis of rotation is tilted to 23.5° from vertical
- a bright light source (lamp with at least a 75-watt bulb and without a shade)
- (optional) photocell such as a mini panel solar cell
- (optional) multimeter or voltmeter

Time

50 minutes

Figure 10.4
Light and globes representing Earth's orbit

SAFETY ALERT

1. Be careful when working with a hot lamp—skin can be burned. Notify your teacher immediately if someone is burned.

2. When working with lamps, keep away from water or other liquids—electrical shock hazard.

3. Make sure all trip and fall hazards are removed from the floor prior to darkening the room for this Activity.

4. Use caution when working with electrical wires—sharp hazard—can cut or puncture skin.

What Can I Do?

Although we often talk about spring arriving with the first robin or when the dogwood blooms, seasons are actually defined astronomically. Scientists need data from far afield to know when organisms migrate or begin to bud or bloom, because their timing is shifting with global climate change. You can help conduct research through programs such as Project Budburst, the Journey North, and the Great Backyard Bird Count. Search for those programs online by their names or, for a more comprehensive list, search for keywords and phrases such as Phenology Observation Programs at *www.usanpn.org/participate/other-programs*.

6. Do the seasons in other parts of the United States differ from the seasons where you live? Why or why not?

7. If you traveled to Australia right now, what season would it be? Explain.

8. What would be necessary for other planets to have seasons as Earth does?

Reasons for the Seasons

What Is Happening?

Earth travels around the Sun in a slightly elliptical orbit. Because of this orbit, Earth's distance from the Sun varies slightly depending on where Earth is in its orbit. Contrary to popular opinion, however, Earth's seasons are only marginally related to this small variation in the planet's distance from the Sun. This is one of the most common preconceptions in astronomy. Mistakenly, people think that when Earth is farthest away from the Sun, it is winter; and when Earth is closest to the Sun, summer occurs. The change in distance is, in fact, not great enough to cause a significant change in temperature. In fact, Earth is closest to the Sun in January, when it is winter in the Northern Hemisphere. Furthermore, if distance from the Sun determined the seasons, then all of Earth should have the same season at the same time. This is not the case. When it is summer in the Northern Hemisphere, it is winter in the Southern Hemisphere.

Instead, the reason Earth has seasons pertains to the angle at which Earth rotates as it revolves around the Sun. Generally, when objects rotate, they rotate around a vertical axis, just like a spinning top or a basketball spinning on someone's finger. Earth, however, rotates around an axis tilted relative to its orbit. The angle of the tilt is 23.5° from vertical (see **Figure 10.5**).

Objective

Understand why Earth has seasons.

Key Concept

III: Earth's characteristic phases and seasons

Materials

The class will need

- one or two globes mounted so that the axis of rotation is tilted to 23.5° from vertical
- a bright light source (lamp with at least a 75-watt bulb and without a shade)
- (optional) photocell such as a mini panel solar cell
- (optional) multimeter or voltmeter

Time

50 minutes

How Do We Know This?

How do we know the tilt of Earth's axis?

Today, astronomers measure the tilt of Earth's axis with incredible accuracy by studying the radio waves received from distant galaxies. Using radio telescopes at different locations on Earth, they measure differences in the arrival of radio signals from things like quasars.

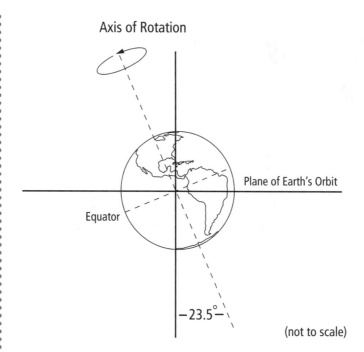

Figure 10.5
Tilt of Earth's axis

Due to this tilt of Earth's rotational axis, rays of sunlight strike parts of Earth more vertically than others. Slanting rays of sunlight heat less intensely than more vertical ones. In summer in the Northern Hemisphere, the North Pole is tilted toward the Sun, as shown in **Figure 10.6**. Therefore, sunlight strikes the Northern Hemisphere more directly in summer, and the weather is warmer.

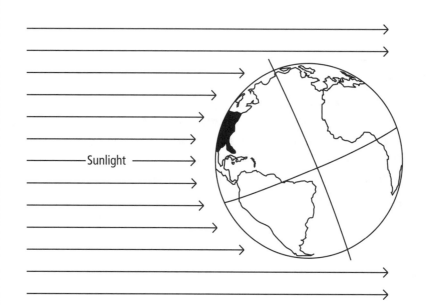

Figure 10.6
Summer in the Northern Hemisphere

In winter, the direction of tilt is the same as in summer, but since Earth is now on the opposite side of the Sun, the Southern Hemisphere is tilted toward the Sun and the Northern Hemisphere is tilted away (see **Figure 10.7**). The rays that strike the Northern Hemisphere slant more and heat less. Fall and spring are simply the points between these two extremes.

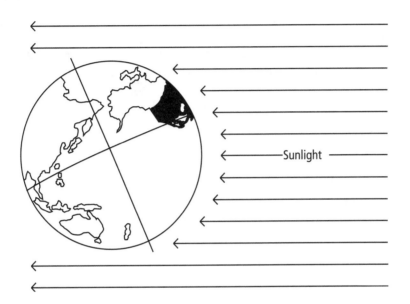

Sunlight

Figure 10.7
Winter in the Northern Hemisphere

The concept of slanted light rays causing less heating than vertical light rays is difficult for students to understand. You may want to add a couple of demonstrations to this Activity to support the development of this concept.

One way to illustrate the effect of the slanting rays concept is to use the optional photocell and multimeter in the Activity as in **Figure 10.8**. The photocell (also known as a mini panel encapsulated solar cell) can be purchased from educational supply companies. A photocell that has a voltage rating of 3–6 v works well. A multimeter (used for measuring voltage) can be purchased at a hardware store. In Positions 1 and 2, place the photocell over the United States, and attach the multimeter leads to the output wires of the photocell. Attach the photocell and the meter as shown in **Figure 10.9**. Students will see that the photocell is receiving and producing more energy in the summer noon position.

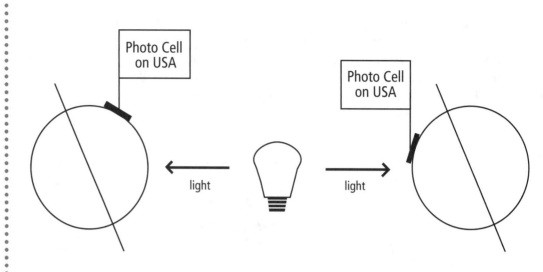

Figure 10.8
Globes, light source, and photocells

Position 1

Position 2

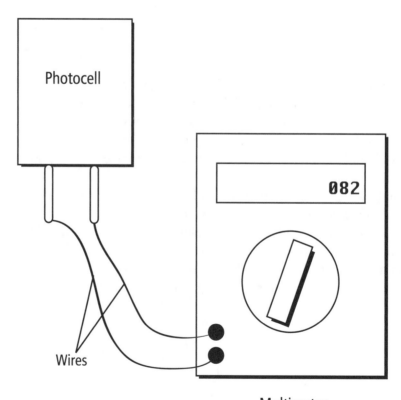

Figure 10.9
Photocell and multimeter

Multimeter

Another way to illustrate the slanted versus vertical rays concept is to project a square grid pattern onto a white exercise ball in a darkened room. Students will see that the squares are smallest directly under the light source—in the middle of the side facing the "Sun." Near the poles and the sunrise and sunset sides, the squares get stretched out. This shows that the surface of Earth is receiving more energy per square meter where the light rays are vertical, and less where they are slanted.

Another consequence of Earth having a tilted axis is that the day's length varies throughout the year. This further contributes to seasonal temperatures; the longer the day, the more energy received from the Sun to warm the atmosphere and the less time for that warmth to dissipate.

This explains seasonal temperature variations, but day-to-day changes are moderated by Earth's atmosphere. That is why the hottest and coldest days of the year rarely occur on the summer and winter solstices respectively.

Preconceptions

Have students write out or sketch their understanding of why seasons occur before doing the Activity. This serves three purposes. First, it gains students' attention. Second, it makes them aware of their own beliefs. Finally, it provides a resource to help you focus instruction on preconceptions that students identify.

What Students Need to Understand

- Earth's distance from the Sun has little to do with the seasons.
- The seasons are caused by Earth's axis of rotation being tilted 23.5° from vertical with respect to its orbital plane.
- Earth's axis always points in the same direction with respect to the stars—over the course of their lifetime.
- When a hemisphere is tilted toward the Sun, summer occurs; when it is tilted away from the Sun, winter occurs there.
- Earth's orbit is only slightly elliptical—not nearly as elliptical as most people think.
- Slanting rays of sunlight do not heat the surface of Earth as much as vertical rays of sunlight.

Time Management

This demonstration should take less than 50 minutes.

Connections

Geologists, climatologists, and oceanographers pay attention to the effect seasons have on icepack and glaciers in our time. But, geologists also study ancient ice ages through ice cores, lake sediments, and glacial features with great names such as kames, kettles, eskers, cols, cirques, roche mountonnée, moraines, arêtes, matterhorns, bergschrunds, varves, and paternoster lakes. Students, especially those learning French or German, might enjoy learning about the features with these names.

Preparation and Procedure

In this Activity, one or two globes and a bright light are used to demonstrate why the seasons occur. Be sure that the light source works. Also, consider acquiring the optional photocell and multimeter as discussed in the What Is Happening? section.

For further information, refer to Reading 12: Reasons for the Seasons.

Extended Learning

- Most textbooks depict Earth's orbit as much more elliptical than it actually is. Students could plot a scale model of Earth's true orbit to see that it more closely resembles a circle than an ellipse. This would enable them to see that distance is not a factor in the seasons. Include instructions on how to draw ellipses of varying eccentricity.

- Students also may be interested in trying to devise a more graphic way of explaining the reason Earth has seasons. It would be informative for students to study other planets to learn if they have seasons. Of particular interest may be the planet Mars, which has a similar tilt (25°), yet has a more eccentric orbit. This results in the seasons being more extreme for the Southern Hemisphere.

Interdisciplinary Study

Seasons are a common theme in music, literature, and art. Encourage students to find all kinds of music (classical, popular, folk) that have references to the seasons. The poem "Winter Moon" by Langston Hughes provides a bridge from astronomy to meteorology. The poem "Seasons" by Evelyn Nitso provides a description of each season.

Differentiated Learning

- For students who struggle with this Activity, we recommend following the suggestions for using a photocell and multimeter, and projecting a grid on a globe described in the What Is Happening? section.

- Students who like mathematics or who think spatially could explore the geometric relationship between cones and ellipses. Have them make cones out of clay and slice through them at various angles to see the shape of the cross sections.

Answers to Student Questions

1. The light should have been brighter on the United States on the globe that had the United States tilted toward the Sun (Position 2).

2. When the United States is tilted away from the light (the Sun), it receives more slanting rays of sunlight, and the light is therefore dimmer.

3. Students should have observed a cycle of increasing and then decreasing intensity, depending on where the globe was originally positioned in the orbit.

4. Winter and summer occur on opposite sides of the light when the intensity of light on the United States is the dimmest and brightest respectively. Fall and spring occur on opposite sides of the light halfway between winter and summer.

5. It might be winter somewhere in the Southern Hemisphere. Chile is an example.

6. Yes. For example, winter in the northeastern part of the United States is much longer and colder than in the southeast. This is because the farther north and south from the equator, the shorter the winter days are. Also, coastal temperatures are moderated by the ocean.

7. It depends on the present season. Generally, it would be the opposite of what the season is in the United States. If it is spring in the United States, it would be fall in Australia. This is because Australia is in the Southern Hemisphere and the United States is in the Northern Hemisphere.

8. Other planets would have to have a tilt in their axes of rotation just as Earth has. It would not have to be a 23.5° tilt, however. They would also require a nearly circular orbit, like Earth's.

Assessment

- Ask students to review and revise their sketches or explanations of seasons.
- You could also ask students to write or draw an explanation for a family member (and even ask for feedback from the family member!).
- For formal assessment, you can grade answers to the questions.

Connections

Have students study Milankovitch cycles and how Earth's orbital variations create the cycles that are responsible for major climate changes, such as ice ages. This leads geologists and climatologists to believe that astronomy ultimately determines the expanse and depth of glacial ice. Search websites such as *www.ncdc. noaa.gov/paleo/milankovitch. html*.

Resources

www.usanpn.org/participate/ other-programs

www.ncdc.noaa.gov/paleo/ milankovitch.html

Activity 11 Summary

Students use Ping-Pong or Styrofoam balls to model the way the Sun illuminates the Moon as the Moon orbits Earth. Then they model the orbit of the Moon around Earth using a painted ball to understand why the Moon shows phases.

Activity	Subject and Content	Objective	Materials
Phases of the Moon	Moon's phases	Understand the cause of the Moon's phases.	For Part 1, the class will need: one bright lamp (at least 75-watt) without shade, one extension cord, one Ping-Pong ball for each student (an option is polystyrene balls), safety glasses or goggles for each student
			For Part 2, each pair of students will need: cardboard, 15-cm diameter Styrofoam ball, pencil, black paint suitable for Styrofoam, safety glasses or goggles for each student

Time	Vocabulary	Key Concept	Margin Features
100 minutes (50 minutes per part)	Phases of the Moon	III: Earth's characteristic phases and seasons	Fast Fact, Safety Alert!, What Can I Do?, Connections, Resources

Scientific Inquiry	Unifying Concepts and Processes	Personal/Social Perspectives
Modeling the causes of the Moon's phases	Effects of the Moon's orbit around Earth and solar illumination	Evaluating preconceptions about Moon phases

Phases of the Moon

Background

Every 29.5 days, the Moon's shape appears to change in a predictable cycle. We call the shapes **phases of the Moon**. For thousands of years, people have recorded these phases and during this time, the cycle has never changed. Even though we know with confidence what the Moon will look like on any day or night of the year, many people cannot explain why the Moon's shape appears to change. Some people say that Earth's shadow falls on the Moon and blocks our view of part of it, as shown in **Figure 11.1**. Others say that clouds block part of the Moon. Both explanations are incorrect.

The physical shape of the Moon never does change. It is always a sphere with millions of craters and other landforms on it. What changes is the portion of the Moon that we can see from Earth. The Sun always illuminates half of the Moon. Sometimes we can see the entire illuminated part of the Moon; this is called a full Moon. Other times, we cannot see any of the illuminated part—a new Moon. And all the stages in between a new and full Moon occur as well. But, why does the shape of the Moon appear to change in this way? It is because the Moon orbits Earth.

This Activity will show how the Moon's orbit causes the Moon's phases.

Vocabulary
Phases of the Moon: The cycle of changes of the portion of the Moon that is visible from Earth.

Fast Fact
In December 1968, from *Apollo 8*, the far side of the Moon was observed directly by human eyes for the first time. Astronauts aboard orbited the moon 10 times on Christmas Eve. They transmitted television images and took a classic, stunning photo of Earth rising over the edge of the Moon.

Objective
Understand the cause of the Moon's phases.

Activity 11

Figure 11.1
Moon orbiting Earth

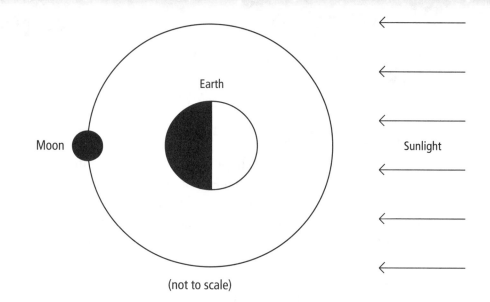

(not to scale)

Materials

For Part 1, the class will need

- one bright lamp (at least 75-watt) without shade
- one extension cord
- one Ping-Pong ball for each student (an option is polystyrene balls)
- safety glasses or goggles for each student

For Part 2, each pair of students will need

- cardboard
- 15-cm diameter Styrofoam ball
- pencil
- black paint suitable for Styrofoam
- safety glasses or goggles for each student

Time

100 minutes
(50 minutes per part)

SAFETY ALERT

1. Safety glasses or goggles are required for this Activity.

2. Be careful when working with a hot lamp—skin can be burned. Notify your teacher immediately if someone is burned.

3. When working with lamps, keep away from water or other liquids—electrical shock hazard.

4. Keep extension cords off the floor—trip and fall hazards.

5. Make sure all trip and fall hazards are removed from the floor prior to darkening the room for this Activity.

Procedure

Part 1

1. Put on eye protection and then place the bright lamp without a lamp shade in the center of a darkened room. Make the room as dark as you can.

2. Each student should have a Ping-Pong ball (a Moon), and the entire class should form a circle around the lamp. This circle should be as tight as possible, yet still allow each student to turn around with one arm extended.

3. You should face the lamp (the Sun) and hold the ball in your left hand directly in front of your body and slightly above your head.

4. Observe what portion of the side of the "Moon" facing you is illuminated by the "Sun."

5. To represent the Moon's orbit around Earth, turn 45° to the left and make the same observation.

6. Continue to make 45° turns until you are once again facing the "Sun." Note that after facing directly away from the "Sun," you will need to hold the ball in your right hand.

Part 2

1. Paint exactly half of the Styrofoam ball black with paint. The simplest way to do this is to cut a hole the diameter of the ball in a piece of cardboard. Putting the ball in that hole before painting it will keep one side protected from the paint. This simulates the Moon with one side illuminated by the Sun and the other side facing away from the Sun. (The Moon is actually all about the same color.)

2. Stick a pencil about 5 cm into the Styrofoam ball as shown in **Figure 11.2**.

3. Stand in an open space and have another student stand about 3 m away facing you and holding the ball at eye level so that you can see the black side only.

4. The student holding the "Moon" should walk around you in a circle; he or she should make sure (1) not to turn the ball, and (2) to face in the same direction at all times. For example, always face the board. The student will have to walk backwards and sideways at times to do this.

5. At each of the eight positions indicated on **BLM 11.1**, draw the portion of the white part of the ball that you can see.

6. Switch places with the student helping you and repeat the Activity.

7. Label your drawings on **BLM 11.1** with a name for each phase of the Moon.

Topic: moon phases
Go to: www.scilinks.org
Code: PSCA107

Figure 11.2
Styrofoam ball mounted on pencil

Questions and Conclusions

Part 1

1. How much of the illuminated part of the ball (Moon) could you see when you were facing the lamp (Sun)?

2. Describe what happened to the illuminated portion of the ball that you could see as the Moon went around you in a circle.

3. Whether you could see it or not, how much of the ball's surface area was always illuminated?

Part 2

4. What fraction of the ball was white (illuminated by the Sun) during the whole Activity?

5. Were you able to see all the white or "illuminated" portion of the ball throughout the Activity?

6. Describe what happened to the white portion of the ball that you could see as the Moon went around you in a circle.

7. If you represent Earth and the ball represents the Moon, describe where in the room the Sun would have been.

What Can I Do?

You can watch the Moon and observe its shape and features. If you draw what you see, you will probably pay closer attention to the features. And, as the line between dark and light sweeps across the moon, different features will stand out more. (The line is called the terminator.) For a breathtaking view, use binoculars or a telescope. Local astronomy clubs and planetariums often have observing sessions for everyone.

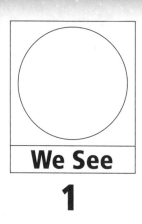

We See

1

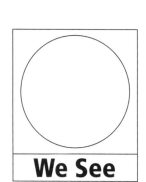

We See

2

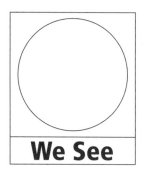

We See

8

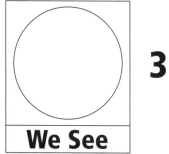

We See

3

7

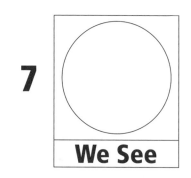

We See

4

We See

5

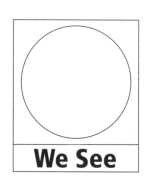

We See

6

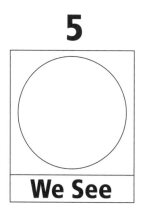

We See

5

Keep this page upright as you draw what you see.

Phases of the Moon

What Is Happening?

Every 29.5 days, the Moon's appearance goes through a predictable cycle of changes. While most people are well aware of the Moon's phases, one of the most common preconceptions in astronomy concerns why these changes in the Moon's apparent shape occur. Perhaps the most prevalent, incorrect explanation for Moon phases is that they are caused by Earth's shadow on the Moon. (This is a lunar eclipse.) Another incorrect explanation is that clouds block part of the Moon.

The correct explanation of the phases of the Moon involves visualizing the relationship among three separate objects, two of which are in motion around the third. Models work best to explain and to visualize this relationship. **Figure 11.3** shows one model of how the Sun, Earth, and Moon interact to produce the phases of the Moon. In this model, the Sun is positioned off the right-hand side of the page. The inner ring of Moons illustrates that half of the Moon is always illuminated—the half facing the Sun. However, depending on where the Moon is in its orbit around Earth, we may see all of the illuminated area, none of it, or any fraction between the two. The outer ring of Moons shows how the Moon would appear in each of eight positions to a person on Earth.

Objective
Understand the cause of the Moon's phases.

Key Concept
III: Earth's characteristic phases and seasons

Materials
For Part 1, the class will need

- one bright lamp (at least 75-watt) without shade
- one extension cord
- one Ping-Pong ball for each student (an option is polystyrene balls)
- safety glasses or goggles for each student

For Part 2, each pair of students will need

- cardboard
- 15-cm diameter Styrofoam ball
- pencil
- black paint suitable for Styrofoam
- safety glasses or goggles for each student

Time
100 minutes
(50 minutes per part)

How Do We Know This?

How do we know that the Moon's orbit around Earth is tilted in relation to Earth's orbit around the Sun?

Ancient skywatchers carefully observed the Moon's position in relation to the stars from one day to the next. By noting the positions of the stars in relation to where the Sun was when it set, they were able to observe the Sun's position in relation to the stars from one day to the next. This allowed them to plot the apparent motions of the Sun and Moon among the stars, which showed the 5° difference in the apparent path of each of these bodies. Observations of eclipses confirms this tilt as well. If the Moon's orbit were not tilted in relation to Earth's orbit around the Sun, we would have both a lunar and solar eclipse each month.

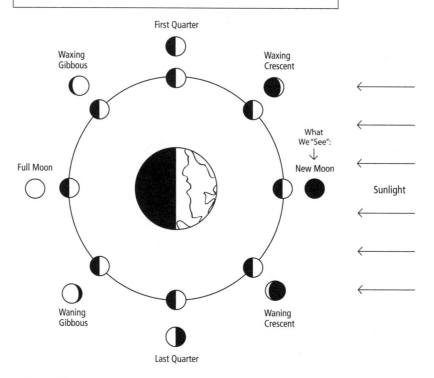

Note:
- Objects are not to scale.
- The inner circle shows a view from above Earth's North Pole.
- The outer circle is the view that we see from Earth.

Figure 11.3
The phases of the Moon

(not to scale)

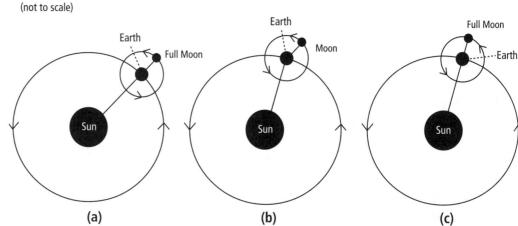

Figure 11.4
(a) Alignment of Sun, Moon, and Earth in full Moon

(b) Alignment of Sun, Earth, and Moon after 27.3 days

(c) Alignment of Sun, Earth, and Moon after two more days (29.5 days total)

(a)   (b)   (c)

This cycle of apparent shapes repeats every 29.5 days. This period of time may seem incorrect since it takes the Moon only 27.3 days to go around Earth once. The difference is explained by the fact that Earth is moving, too. **Figures 11.4a–c** illustrate this. **Figure 11.4a** shows the alignment of the Sun, Moon, and Earth during the full Moon. After 27.3 days (**Figure 11.4b**), the Moon has made one complete orbit around Earth, but Earth has moved in its own orbit, too. Because of this, it takes about two more days before the Moon is back in a position relative to Earth to appear full. At that point, the cycle of phases begins again (**Figure 11.4c**).

This Activity is designed to show that the reason for the changes in the visible shape of the Moon is the motion of the Moon around Earth. Some students will probably question why a lunar eclipse does not occur once a month when the Moon is on the opposite side of Earth from the Sun, or why a solar eclipse does not happen once a month when the Moon passes in front of the Sun. The plane of the Moon's orbit is slightly tilted (as shown in **Figure 11.5**); this tilt precludes a monthly eclipse from occurring. It is important to help students make the connection between what happens in this Activity and reality. Questions such as "Where are the Sun, Moon, and Earth when the Moon is in the first quarter?" require students to transfer their thinking from the model to reality.

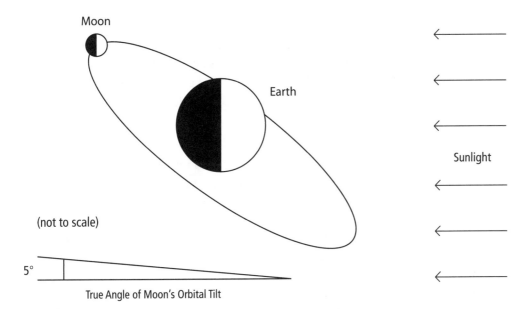

Moon

Earth

Sunlight

(not to scale)

5°

True Angle of Moon's Orbital Tilt

Figure 11.5
The tilted plane of the Moon's orbit

Preconceptions

At the beginning of the Activity, ask students to write their own explanation of why the shape of the Moon appears to change. Encourage them to use diagrams in their explanation. This exercise helps you be aware of specific misconceptions that students may have.

What Students Need to Understand

- Half of the Moon is always illuminated.
- The actual shape of the Moon does not change, only the portion of the illuminated side that can be seen from Earth.
- The cycle of changes in the apparent shape of the Moon is due to the Moon orbiting Earth.

- The changes in the apparent shape of the Moon occur in a predictable cycle, which repeats every 29.5 days.
- The plane of the Moon's orbit is slightly tilted, and this precludes monthly eclipses.

Time Management

Including setup, this Activity should take 50 minutes for each part.

Preparation and Procedure

Part 1

Be sure to have one Ping-Pong ball for each student and check that the lamp works. You might need to divide the class into two groups for students to stand close enough to the light and yet have enough room to rotate with one arm outstretched. However, only one group can work at a time.

For further information, refer to Reading 13: Phases of the Moon.

Part 2

Painting the Styrofoam balls is a messy task, so you may want to do this for students. Tempera or acrylic paint works best. Some spray paint dissolves Styrofoam. You need to prepare only one class set.

Be sure beforehand that there is enough room for all students to work at once. It is helpful to mark off work spaces prior to the class. Students will work in pairs in this Activity. You may want to pair up students prior to the class in order to save time.

It is important that students move the Styrofoam balls correctly when walking around the observer. One side of the Moon must always face in the same direction, toward a wall or the chalkboard, for example. The ball must not rotate. You should demonstrate the correct movement for students. If done correctly, the larger size of the Styrofoam ball will allow students to understand how what they can see of the illuminated side of the Moon becomes the new, waxing, full, and waning Moon that they see in the sky.

Important note: This Activity may perpetuate some preconceptions that students already have about the Moon. You should point these out to students; make it clear that this Activity is only a model that shows how a half-illuminated sphere may take on different appearances depending on the relative positions of the sphere and the observer. Students should be made to realize that this model is inaccurate in the following ways: First, the Moon is not colored half-white and half-black as is the Styrofoam ball. Second, the same side of the Moon is not always illuminated. At different times in the cycle of phases, all parts of the Moon become illuminated. Finally, the Moon rotates

SAFETY ALERT

1. Safety glasses or goggles are required for this Activity.

2. Be careful when working with a hot lamp—skin can be burned. Notify your teacher immediately if someone is burned.

3. When working with lamps, keep away from water or other liquids—electrical shock hazard.

4. Keep extension cords off the floor—trip and fall hazards.

5. Make sure all trip and fall hazards are removed from the floor prior to darkening the room for this Activity.

as it orbits Earth, whereas the Styrofoam ball in this Activity does not. It is this rotation of the Moon that causes the same side of the Moon always to face Earth, and it allows all parts of the Moon to be illuminated at different times in the cycle.

Extended Learning

• Students can use these Activities to dispel two common preconceptions about the Moon. People often believe that the same side of the Moon is always illuminated since the same side always faces Earth. The first Activity best demonstrates that this is not true. Another preconception many people have is that since the same side of the Moon always faces Earth, the Moon must not rotate. In the first Activity, if students make a mark on the ball, and take care to always have that mark facing them, they can see that even though the same side of the Ping-Pong ball always faces them, the ball is rotating nonetheless.

Care must be taken, if you choose to do Part 2, not to perpetuate these preconceptions. This is very important.

• Here is another short activity that may further help dispel these preconceptions. Have two students stand 2 m apart facing each other. One student represents Earth and the other the Moon. Designate a third student to stand in one spot to the side of the other two and mimic the motion of the person being the Moon (see **Figure 11.6**). Have the student representing the Moon walk side-step in a circle around the other student, facing him or her at all times. In this way, the same side of the student representing the Moon is always facing "Earth." As the "Moon" is going around "Earth," the third student stays in one spot but will have to turn his or her body to face the same way as the "Moon." This should demonstrate to students that even though the same side of the Moon always faces Earth, the Moon still rotates and hence the same side could not always be illuminated by the Sun.

• Observing the Moon in the daytime also works to dispel and prevent certain preconceptions. Some people think the Moon is visible only at night. Observing the Moon in the day not only helps to eliminate this preconception, but it also helps students transfer what they have learned in this Activity to the actual Sun-Earth-Moon relationships. Note: If students go out in the morning when the Moon is near the last quarter phase, and they hold a Ping-Pong ball up near where they see the Moon in the sky, they will see the same phase on the ball! For more information on daytime Moon calendars, go to *http://planetarium-web.madison.k12.wi.us/mooncal/daymoon*.

• Going beyond the concepts addressed directly, this Activity is a good starting point for students to explore the difference between a lunar eclipse and a new Moon, and to learn the names of the phases of the Moon. They can also learn why we do not have eclipses every lunar cycle. It is also an opportunity to discuss the moons of other planets. Students can also learn and explain why Venus has phases.

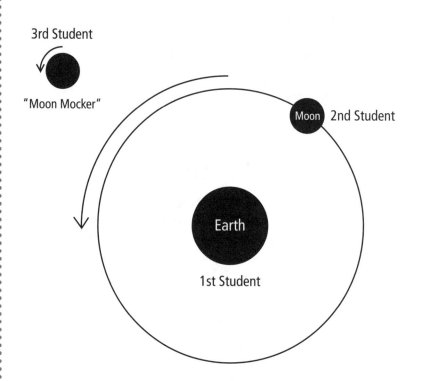

Figure 11.6
Students acting as Earth, Moon, and "Moon Mocker"

Interdisciplinary Study

- Through the ages, the phases of the Moon and lunar eclipses have been a source of myth and folklore. It is only in the last few centuries that phases and eclipses have been correctly explained. (Actually, the ancient Greeks had phases and eclipses figured out, although they, of course, did not think of the Earth moving but of the Sun and Moon orbiting Earth. The effect is the same—you still get phases and eclipses.) Different cultures have explained these phenomena in different ways. Comparing these cultures and their explanations would be an interesting interdisciplinary project.

- Native Americans (such as the Miami Tribe of Oklahoma) marked the progression of time and seasonal environmental changes with a lunar calendar. Students could learn the names of full Moons and the reasons behind the names for full Moons used by different tribes. They could analyze similarities and differences among the Moons' names.

- The phases of the Moon have also found their way into poetry. Langston Hughes's "Winter Moon" and Myra Cohn Livingston's "Moon" are two examples. Students may have heard or read the phrase "blue Moon." Encourage them to find out what it means when someone says that something happens "once in a blue Moon." ("Blue Moon" refers to the occurrence of two full Moons in the same calendar month, something that happens only once or twice a year.) Ask students to find specific references to the blue Moon in music and literature.

- For many people, the Moon in all of its phases is a thing of great beauty and wonder. As such, it has been the source of inspiration for art, literature, and music. Encourage students to listen for references to the Moon in their favorite music. Challenge them to find preconceptions about the Moon in these songs.

Differentiated Learning

This Activity uses a physical model to teach all students. To supplement the experience, direct students to Windows to the Universe. Both English and Spanish readers can choose beginning, intermediate, and advanced reading levels. Search for "Windows Universe" at *www.windows2universe.org*.

Answers to Student Questions

Part 1

1. None or almost none. This is the new Moon.

2. The amount of detail may vary, but it could include the following:

    1st turn—25% of the illuminated portion of the Moon was visible, corresponding to the waxing crescent phase

    2nd turn—50%—first quarter

    3rd turn—75%—waxing gibbous

    4th turn—100%—full Moon

    5th turn—75%—waning gibbous

    6th turn—50%—third quarter

    7th turn—25%—waning crescent

    8th turn—0%—new Moon

3. Fifty percent of the ball was always illuminated.

Part 2

4. Half of the ball was white, even though it could not all be seen all the time.

5. No.

6. Assuming the student started with the black side facing him or her, none of the white would have been visible initially. As the Moon moved, a crescent would have first appeared, then a half, then three-quarters, then a full Moon. As the Moon continued to move, this pattern would have reversed until only the black side was visible again.

7. This will vary for each student. The Sun should be in a position to illuminate the white half of the ball.

Connections

The Moon causes our tides. That is critically important to oceanographers, but it is also significant to meteorologists faced with forecasting a hurricane's potential effects on land. If you teach at the coast, ask students to monitor both the Moon and the tides for at least a month. If a hurricane is threatening your region, ask students to watch the timing of its arrival and the tides.

Connections

If you do not live at the shore, beach, sound, coast, or bay, you can monitor the tide virtually through a webcam (e.g., the Monterey Bay Aquarium's webcam). Search for "Monterey Bay Aquarium," and look under Animals & Activities at *www.montereybayaquarium.org/*.

Alternatively, the National Data Buoy Center provides real-time tidal data for buoys on all coasts. Search for "National Data Buoy Center" at *www.ndbc.noaa.gov/*. Look for data listed as Tides or Water Level.

Resources

www.montereybayaquarium.org

www.ndbc.noaa.gov

www.windows2universe.org

http://planetariumweb.madison.k12.wi.us/mooncal/daymoon

Assessment

- You can ask students to return to their responses in the Preconceptions section and redo or revise how they explained phases of the Moon.
- You can ask students to create a video or web page explaining lunar phases to students in other classes or their family.
- You can grade students' answers to questions.

Readings

Introduction

The following Readings provide background information on the underlying concepts in the Activities included in this book. The Readings go beyond what is found in the background information in the Activities. They can be used as supplementary information for the teacher, or to enhance classroom discussions.

Angular Diameters Reading

Measuring diameters of objects in the solar system presents just as big a problem as measuring distances. Since we cannot measure the size directly, we use a technique that measures the angular diameter.

Figure R1.1 shows an example of an angular diameter. If you could take one piece of string and stretch it from where you are all the way to the right side of the Moon, and then stretch another piece of string to the left side of the Moon from the same starting point, the angle between those two pieces of string would be ½°.

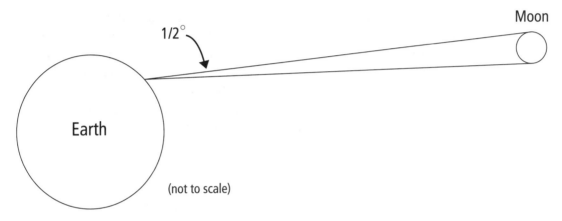

Figure R1.1 Pieces of string are stretched from your location on Earth to each side of the Moon.

It is possible for two objects to have the same angular diameter, even if they are not the same size. Hold your thumb in front of one eye while closing the other. Move your thumb closer to your eye or farther away until it just blocks your view of someone else's head. You know that your thumb is not as big as the person's head, so how can your thumb block the view? The reason is that both your thumb and the person's head have the same angular diameter at that point where one blocks the other, even though they are not the same size. When two objects have the same angular diameter, they have the same apparent size; that is, they appear to be the same size. You will also notice that when your thumb is closer to your eyes, it appears larger than at arm's length.

The apparent size of an object relates to how close or far away it is. Take a coin and place it on a piece of paper. Make a pencil dot 7 cm to the left of the coin. Draw two lines that go from the dot to either side of the coin as shown in **Figure R1.2**.

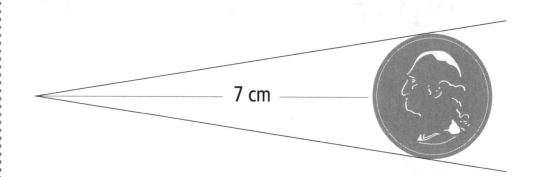

Figure R1.2
Draw two lines from a dot
7 cm from the coin, and
observe the angle.

7 cm

Now move the coin about a centimeter to the right and draw the two lines again from the same point. Move the coin farther to the right and draw the lines. Notice that as the coin is moved farther away, the angle gets smaller. If you viewed the coin from the dot, the apparent size would continually decrease.

Angular diameters are only useful if the distance to the object is known. An object's true diameter can be calculated from its distance and its angular diameter by two different methods. One method involves using an equation from geometry:

$s = r(q/57)$ where
s = true diameter of the object
r = distance to the object (must be in same unit as "s")
q = angular diameter of the object in degrees
57 = conversion factor of radians to degrees

This is true for small angles. Unfortunately, the angular diameter of most objects of interest in astronomy, including planets, is ½° or less, and such angles are hard to measure with commonly available equipment. The second method does not require expensive equipment but does require knowledge of similar triangles.

The relevant features of similar triangles can be illustrated with the following exercise. Using a protractor, draw two lines on a piece of paper to make an acute angle—which is an angle of less than 90°—(the angle in **Figure R1.3** is 53°). On one line, start at the point of intersection and make a mark every 3 cm for 12 cm. On the other line, start at the same point and make a dot every 5 cm for 15 cm. Connect the dots as shown in **Figure R1.3**. You have now made a series of triangles that all have one angle in common, angle X. In this diagram, angle X is 53°. Measure angles A, B, and C in your drawing using a protractor. Are they the same? Measure angles D, E, and F. Are they the same? When all the corresponding angles are equal like this, then the triangles are similar. Similar triangles have another interesting feature. Measure lines XD and XE and divide the first by the second. Now measure lines DA and EB and divide the first by the second. You should get the same, or nearly the same, answer for both. This feature of similar triangles is essential in using angular diameters to determine true diameters of planets in the solar system.

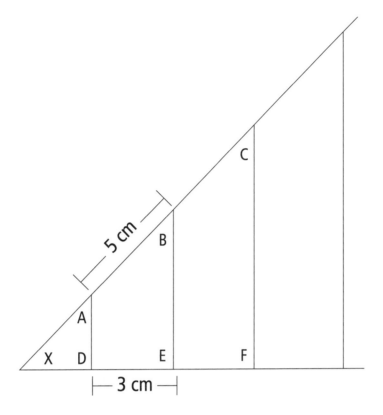

Figure R1.3
This exercise illustrates the relevant features of similar triangles.

Figure R1.4 shows how a coin and the principles of similar triangles can be used to calculate the diameter of the Moon. Once the coin is moved to a point where it just blocks out the view of the full Moon, the two have the same angular diameter. Since they have the same angular diameter, two similar triangles exist, ABC and ADE. The distance to the coin (AB) and its diameter (BC) are easily measured. The distance to the Moon (AD) is known from past measurements. Therefore, the diameter of the Moon (DE) can be calculated by solving the ratio AB/AD = BC/DE for DE. Again, this is possible because of the similar triangles that exist when the two objects have the same angular diameter.

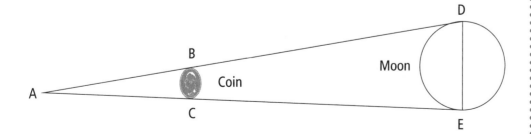

Figure R1.4
Use a coin and similar triangles to calculate the diameter of the Moon.

What Is a Light Year?

The fact that Earth is the only inhabited planet in this solar system is well established. There are, however, innumerable other stars besides the Sun, and astronomers have discovered hundreds of planets orbiting other stars. (You can stay up-to-date on extrasolar planets at *http://planetquest.jpl.nasa.gov.*)

The distances to these stars are immense. Their light takes many years to reach us here on Earth. These stars are being studied now, and one of the fundamental facts to be determined is their distance. Typical units such as miles and kilometers are awkward to measure such distances; therefore, a unit known as the light year is used.

Which number is easier to understand and work with: 5,840 days or 16 years? Both represent the same amount of time. Most people would choose 16 years because smaller numbers are easier to understand. Distances in the universe are more difficult to comprehend or imagine when they are measured in units such as kilometers or miles. This led scientists to develop a new unit of measurement that makes the astronomical distances more manageable—the light year.

The concept of a light year is sometimes difficult to understand partly because of the words themselves. The term light year uses what is normally thought of as a time unit, the year, to measure a distance. But, time units are often used to talk about distances. People often talk about how far it is to some destination by describing how long it takes to get there. As an example, it takes about four hours to fly from the East Coast to the West Coast. Although a time unit is being used, distance is actually being represented.

A light year is defined as the distance that light travels in one Earth year. Light moves extremely fast, 300 thousand km/sec. In one second, light can travel around Earth more than seven times. Nothing travels faster; light is the speed limit. In 31 million seconds—or one year—light will travel a distance of 9.46 trillion km, or almost 240 million times around Earth. This distance equals one light year, abbreviated *ly*.

Distances in the universe are so large that it helps to express them in the scale of light years. Consider the distance to the star Sirius—more than 81 trillion km. That is a huge number to comprehend. Using the light year as the unit of measurement, the distance becomes only 8.6 ly—much easier to work with. The light year is an appropriate unit to measure vast distances.

The speed of light makes everything appear to happen instantly in our everyday experience. When we watch a soccer game and see someone kick the ball, we assume that the ball was kicked right then, not five minutes before we saw it. For all practical purposes, we are safe in that assumption because light travels so fast. For us to see the soccer ball, we must see the light that is being reflected from it, and it does take time for the light to travel from the ball to our eyes. However, the amount of time is far too short to measure. If the distance from the ball to our eyes were 10 m, the light reflecting off the ball would take only 300 millionths of a second to reach our eyes.

Stars are millions and millions of kilometers away. To see a star, that star's light must travel across space to our eyes. The time required for light to travel such a huge distance is easily measured. If the star is 5 ly away, then the light we are seeing from that star took five years to travel to our eyes. It also means that what we see happening at that star is actually what happened five years ago, not what is happening in the star's present. If we see a flare from the star's surface, we are seeing an event that happened five years ago.

Imagine that there is a planet with people on it that is 60 ly away from Earth. The year on Earth is 2002. These people have an extremely powerful telescope and can actually make out the details of what is happening on Earth. If they aim their telescope at Europe, they will see World War II being fought, since it was happening 60 years ago. They will not see the events of 2002 on Earth until the year 2062.

Even though it may seem frustrating that we cannot see what is happening to a star right now, tens, hundreds, or even thousands of years is a small fraction of the life of a star. Also, astronomers and cosmologists who study the evolution of galaxies can use vast distances to travel back in time virtually. Using powerful telescopes, such as the Hubble Space Telescope, astronomers can observe galaxies that are 13 billion light years away. This allows them to see what the earliest galaxies were like long ago.

Hubble Space Telescope

Throughout history, humans have looked to the night sky with awe and wonder. Until a mere 400 years ago, all of our knowledge of the universe came from capturing light with the unaided eye. Then, a new tool, the telescope, revolutionized our understanding of our place in the universe by allowing us to gather more light, and magnify the view. Over the past four centuries, telescopes have grown in size and improved in quality; however, moisture and dust in the Earth's atmosphere limits the ability of Earth-based telescopes.

Delivered to its orbit 600 km above Earth's surface by the space shuttle *Discovery* in 1990, the Hubble Space Telescope can detect light before it can be absorbed or distorted by the atmosphere. Hubble was not the first space telescope, but one of the largest. It is a reflecting telescope with a mirror 2.4 m wide. It is the size of a large school bus, and weighs as much as two full-grown elephants. As the only telescope designed to be serviced in space by astronauts, it is also the most versatile, hosting 13 scientific instruments. Five teams of astronauts, from 1993 to 2009, visited the Hubble telescope to make repairs and install new instruments, making the telescope 100 times more powerful than when it was first launched. The various instruments have allowed Hubble to observe using not only visible light, but also near infrared and ultraviolet.

In its first 20 years, Hubble observed over 30,000 celestial targets, and amassed an archive of over a half-million pictures. Hubble's Ultra Deep Field image, the most detailed visible light image ever made of some of the farthest objects in the universe, contains an estimated 10,000 galaxies. Yet, it only covers a small fraction of the sky, equal to one-tenth the diameter of the full Moon. The most distant galaxies in the image are over 13 billion light years away. Since it takes time for light to travel through space, as we see farther and farther objects, we are also looking farther and farther back in time. So, we are seeing the way galaxies looked 13 billion years ago. This Hubble Ultra Deep Field reveals some of the first galaxies in the history of the universe.

Hubble's accomplishments include helping cosmologists to refine their estimate of the age of the universe to 13.7 billion years; revealing that nearly all galaxies contain supermassive black holes at their core; helping astronomers determine how planets form; surprising scientists with the discovery that the expansion of the universe is speeding up due to something cosmologists are calling "dark energy"; and more.

Even though advances in technology make it possible for ground-based telescopes to rival the quality of space-based telescopes, they still cannot completely offset the absorbing and distorting effects of the atmosphere. The Hubble Space Telescope has revolutionized our understanding of the nature and evolution of the universe, captured the imagination of curious observers around the world, and laid the foundation for the next generation of space telescopes.

Scale Measurements

Using parallax (see Reading 6) and angular diameters (see Reading 1) are two ways of measuring the distance to and size of objects in the solar system. The scale model is another method of indirect measurement used in astronomy and other Earth sciences as well.

Everyone has seen a model of something: cars, airplanes, buildings, and spacecraft, for example. You can use these models to determine what the measurements would be on the real thing. As long as the measurement of any one part of the real object is known, the rest of the measurements can be determined from the model.

For example, suppose the tire on a scale model car has a diameter of 2 cm, and on the real car the tire measures 60 cm in diameter. This means that 2 cm on the model represents 60 cm on the real car (or, dividing each measurement by 2, then 1 cm on the model represents 30 cm on the real car). This is all that is required to determine all the measurements on the real car from the model. If the model is 20 cm long, then the car must be 20 × 30 or 600 cm long. If the model is 7.5 cm wide, how wide is the car? If the model is 2.5 cm high, how high is the car?

The same technique can be applied to the solar system. If a scale model is drawn on a piece of paper, then only one true distance must be found to calculate all the others. Nicolaus Copernicus published his scale model of the solar system out to Saturn almost 500 years ago.

Each of these methods—parallax, angular diameters, and scale models—is used to determine where Earth is in the solar system, where the other planets are, and the size of each object. Such information is essential to grasp the significance of the unique aspects of Earth.

If Earth were much closer to the Sun, its oceans—the birthplace of life—would have boiled away long ago. Earth is the only planet in the solar system with liquid oceans. The plants that came into existence because of the oceans, and the oceans themselves, moderate the amount of carbon dioxide in the atmosphere. Without these, Earth would have developed a runaway greenhouse effect (a topic discussed in greater detail later), increasing the average temperature to hundreds of degrees Celsius. In this sense, it would have been similar to Venus, which is devoid of life.

If Earth were farther from the Sun, all the water that is in the oceans now would be frozen, again depriving it of one of the necessities for life, liquid water. Had this happened, Earth would resemble Mars more closely, another planet found to have no life.

The facts of Earth's location and size are the beginning points to understanding what makes Earth unique and why it is the only planet in the solar system that sustains life. These facts only become apparent when Earth is placed in the context of the rest of the solar system. The comparisons that then arise between Earth and the other planets lead to a greater appreciation of our place in the solar system and the universe.

The Goldilocks Effect: Earth Is Just Right

So far, scientists have found that Earth is the only planet in the solar system capable of sustaining life as we know it—that is, complex, multicellular life-forms similar to human beings.

The Goldilocks Principle refers to a planet such as Earth that is "just right" for sustaining human life. The popular term, Goldilocks Principle, or Effect, comes from the traditional folk tale, "The Story of the Three Bears" (or "Goldilocks and the Three Bears"), first published in Britain in the 1830s. The idea of something being "just right" comes from this story, in which Goldilocks finds three bowls of porridge, one that is too hot, another too cold, and a third that is just right. And so it goes for three chairs, one too big, the next too small, and the other just right. Then, being tired, Goldilocks finds three beds, one is too hard, the next is too soft, and the final is just right.

The idea of "just right" has come to mean something that is in the middle, between two extremes, like Goldilocks' bowls of porridge, chairs, and beds.

In terms of astronomy, the Goldilocks Principle refers to planets that are Earth-like and thus habitable by complex, multicellular life-forms such as humans. The scientific term is the habitable zone (HZ) (**Figure R5.1**). This generally refers to the distance a planet (such as Earth) is from the star (such as our Sun), where a planet can maintain liquid water on its surface.

For example, the two planets closest to Earth in the solar system are Venus and Mars. Both have many similarities to Earth but neither has been found to support life.

Venus is the second planet from the Sun in our solar system (Mercury is the closest), and Earth's neighbor. Venus is similar to Earth in size and composition, but its atmosphere is quite different. Venus's thick atmosphere, composed mostly of carbon dioxide, and total cloud cover trap in the heat, making Venus the hottest planet in the solar system. The surface of the planet is so hot—nearly 500°C—that any water that might have existed would have been completely vaporized.

Mars, the fourth planet from the Sun, Earth's neighbor on the other side, has some similarities to Earth and to Venus (see Activity 9: Comparing Earth to Mars and Venus). Like Venus, most of Mars's atmosphere is made up of carbon dioxide, with trace amounts of methane and water. Mars is known as the Red Planet because of the iron oxide in its atmosphere, but that atmosphere is so thin, it cannot protect the planet's surface and trap heat with its greenhouse gases. As a result, the surface temperature of Mars is very cold, as low as –90°C.

Earth remains the "just right" planet because of its distance from the Sun, and its atmosphere that traps and retains the right amount of heat to allow liquid water to exist. These are some of the reasons Earth is just right to sustain human life.

The concept of the HZ leads inevitably to the question of other life in the universe. There are a great many planetary systems in the Milky Way galaxy, and odds are good that some of these planets will be in the HZ. Such Goldilocks planets may have conditions similar to Earth with the proper atmosphere, liquid water, and habitable temperatures.

Planets outside our solar system are known as extrasolar planets, or exoplanets. Scientists have already identified hundreds of exoplanets. Astronomers are tirelessly searching for Earth-like planets. Perhaps there is life on other Goldilocks planets.

Figure R5.1
This graphic shows the relationship of the mass (and luminosity) of a star to the distance of the star's habitable zone.

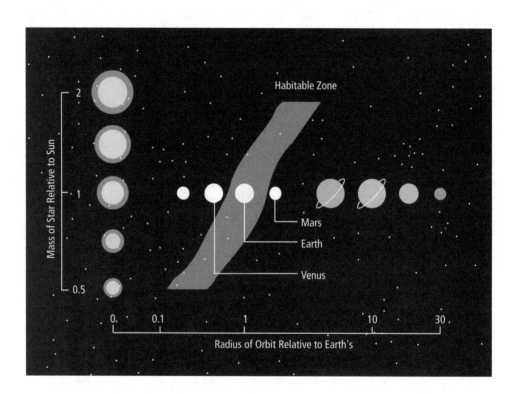

The Parallax Effect Reading

There are two ways to measure distance, directly and indirectly. When we use a tape measure or a meter stick and measure a distance, we are making a direct measurement. If we look at two chairs across the room, compare their relative sizes, and then infer which chair is closer, we are measuring indirectly. Now consider distances on a much larger scale—like those of the solar system. Imagine being faced with the task of using ordinary rulers and scales to measure the circumference of Earth or the distance from Earth to Venus. To find out how big the other planets are and how far away they are, we must use forms of indirect measurement. Three common methods are scale measurement (see Reading 4), measurement by parallax (see Reading 6), and angular diameter (see Reading 1).

One of the methods of indirect measurement takes advantage of the parallax effect. To demonstrate this phenomenon, hold your thumb in front of you at arm's length and look at it with one eye. Line it up with something in the background, such as a tree. Without moving your thumb or your head, look at it with your other eye. Notice that your thumb appears to have moved against the background (see **Figure R6.1**). This apparent change of position against background objects when viewed from different points of observation is called the parallax effect. Each of our eyes is a different point of observation; therefore, we experience a parallax.

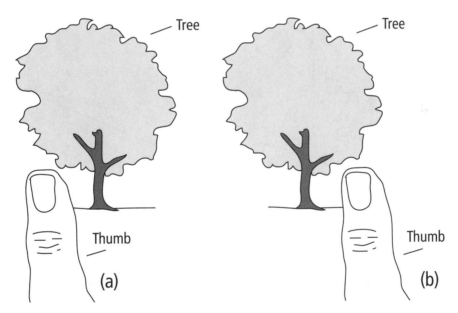

Figure R6.1 This figure shows the parallax effect, the apparent movement of an object from different points. In (a), only the right eye is open, and the tree appears to the right of the thumb. In (b), the left eye is open, and the tree appears to the left of the thumb.

Several factors affect parallax. Two major factors are the distance between the observer and the object being observed, and the distance between the two points of observation, called the baseline. The baseline must be known if parallax is to provide a useful measurement of distance. In the example above, the baseline was the distance between your two eyes. The fact that there is a distance between our eyes makes it possible to judge distance by parallax. Our depth perception is dramatically reduced when we use only one eye. A criterion for accurately judging distance by parallax, though, is that the observer must be so far away from the *background* objects that there is no measurable parallax effect for them.

The baseline and the distance to the object affect parallax in opposite ways. As the baseline increases, parallax increases and is more useful for measuring distances. For this reason, larger baselines are always desired. As the distance to the object increases, the parallax decreases. Therefore, the farther away an object is, the more difficult it is to measure its parallax and the greater the need to have a large baseline. This phenomenon explains why stars all look equidistant to the naked eye.

To measure the distance to some of the closest stars, the required baseline is the diameter of Earth's orbit around the Sun (149 million km), hence the period between the two observations is six months (see **Figure R6.2**). The actual calculation of the distance to a star uses the parallax angle, which is one-half of the apparent change in its angular position.

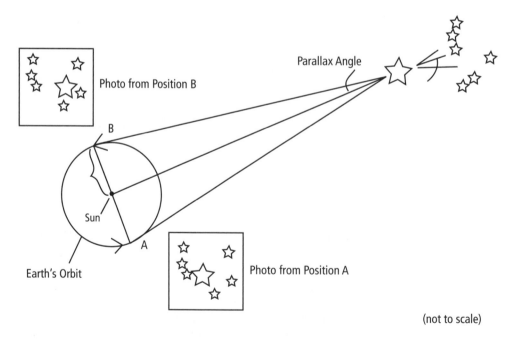

Figure R6.2
Measuring the distance to a star using the parallax angle

Photo from Position B

Parallax Angle

B

Sun

A

Earth's Orbit

Photo from Position A

(not to scale)

Earth as a System

Our planet Earth is a complex structure or system in which all the parts interact and influence each other, much as the parts of the human body have effects on other parts. So, dental problems can have an impact well beyond the mouth where they occur. For example, inflammation from gum disease can lead to other health problems elsewhere in the body, such as heart attacks and strokes.

The four major subsystems of Earth are (1) air, (2) land, (3) water, and (4) life. These are known scientifically as atmosphere (air), lithosphere (land), hydrosphere (water), and biosphere (life). These four systems interact and help sustain one another. For example, when water is heated by the Sun, it evaporates into the air and then falls on land as precipitation (rain, snow, etc.). An abundance of rain leads to dense forests and jungles, such as the Amazonian rain forest or the Central African jungle. On the other hand, a lack of rain leads to dry, nearly lifeless deserts, such as the Mojave Desert in the western United States, the Sahara in Africa, or Antarctica.

A drastic change in one of the subsystems leads to consequences in others. For example, changes in the biosphere can affect the other systems, such as the lithosphere. In many cases, man (in the biosphere) has created changes through his actions. As an example, Madagascar, not too long ago, was almost completely covered with dense forests that supported an immense variety of plant and animal species. But, in the push for exports such as beef and coffee, huge areas of the rain forest were cut down or burned to make way for agriculture.

Today, only about one-third of the original rain forest remains, which has led to the loss of topsoil through erosion and, even more disastrously, the decline in the diversity of plants and animal species on the island.

Similarly, the Industrial Revolution has had an enormous impact on Earth's various systems. Air pollution in the form of additional carbon dioxide and other gases in Earth's atmosphere have led to increased temperatures. For example, the Intergovernmental Panel on Climate Change (IPCC), which is made up of 1,300 scientists from the United States and around the world, estimates that average temperatures will rise between 2°C and 5°C (2.5°F and 10°F) over the next century. We are already seeing the effects of this climate change in the form of retreating glaciers and receding ice caps in the Arctic. With the melting ice comes rising sea levels and threats to low-lying areas around the world.

All of Earth's systems are interrelated, so that rising temperatures will have impacts on the other subsystems as well. For more information and the most recent data on global climate change, visit the NASA website at *http://climate.nasa.gov/effects*.

Global Warming

Over the last five years, 600 scientists from the Intergovernmental Panel on Climate Change sifted through thousands of studies about global warming published in forums ranging from scientific journals to industry publications and distilled the world's accumulated knowledge into this conclusion: "Warming of the climate system is unequivocal."

Far from being some future fear, global warming is happening now, and scientists have evidence that humans are to blame. For decades, cars and factories have spewed billions of tons of greenhouse gases into the atmosphere, and these gases caused temperatures to rise between 0.6°C and 0.9°C (1.08°F to 1.62°F) over the past century. The rate of warming in the last 50 years was double the rate observed over the last 100 years. Temperatures are certain to go up further.

But, why should we worry about a seemingly small increase in temperature? It turns out that the global average temperature is quite stable over long periods of time, and small changes in that temperature correspond to enormous changes in the environment. For example, during the last ice age, when ice sheets a mile thick covered North America all the way down to the northern states, the world was only 9–15°F colder than today. Much of modern human civilization owes its existence to the stability in the average global temperature since the end of the last ice age—a stability that allowed human cultures to transition from roaming, hunter–gatherer societies into more permanent, agriculture-supported communities. Even the temperature change of a degree or two that has occurred over the last century is capable of producing significant changes in our environment and way of life.

In the future, it is very likely that rising temperatures will lead to more frequent heat waves, and virtually certain that the seas will rise, which could leave low-lying nations awash in seawater. Warmer temperatures will alter weather patterns, making it likely that there will be more intense droughts and more intense rain events. Moreover, global warming will last thousands of years. To gain an understanding of how global warming might impact humanity, it is necessary to understand what global warming is, how scientists measure it, and how forecasts for the future are made.

What Is Global Warming?

Global warmth begins with sunlight. When light from the Sun reaches Earth, roughly 30% of it is reflected back into space by clouds, atmospheric particles, reflective ground surfaces, and even ocean surf. The remaining 70% of the light is absorbed by the land, air, and oceans, heating our planet's surface and atmosphere and making life on Earth possible. Solar energy does not stay bound up in Earth's environment forever. Instead, as the rocks, the air, and the sea warm, they emit thermal radiation, or infrared heat. Much of this thermal radiation travels directly out to space, allowing Earth to cool.

Some of this outgoing radiation, however, is reabsorbed by water vapor, carbon dioxide, and other gases in the atmosphere (called greenhouse gases because of their heat-trapping capacity) and is then reradiated back toward Earth's surface. On the whole, this reabsorption process is good. If there were no greenhouse gases or clouds in the atmosphere, Earth's average surface temperature would be a very chilly –18°C (0°F) instead of the comfortable 15°C (59°F) that it is today.

What has scientists concerned now is that over the past 250 years, humans have been artificially raising the concentration of greenhouse gases in the atmosphere at an ever-increasing rate. By 2004, humans were pumping out over 8 billion tons of carbon dioxide per year. Some of it was absorbed by "sinks" like forests or the ocean, and the rest accumulated in the atmosphere. We produce millions of pounds of methane by allowing our trash to decompose in landfills and by breeding large herds of methane-belching cattle. Nitrogen-based fertilizers and other soil management practices lead to the release of nitrous oxide into the atmosphere.

Once these greenhouse gases get into the atmosphere, they stay there for decades or longer. According to the Intergovernmental Panel on Climate Change (IPCC), since the Industrial Revolution began in about 1750, carbon dioxide levels have increased 35% and methane levels have increased 148%. Paleoclimate readings taken from ice cores and fossil records show that these gases, two of the most abundant greenhouse gases, are at their highest levels in at least the past 650,000 years. Scientists have very high confidence (a phrase the IPCC translates to "greater than 90% certainty") that the increased concentrations of greenhouse gases have made it more difficult for thermal radiation to leave Earth, and as a result, Earth has warmed.

Evidence for Global Warming

Recent observations of warming support the theory that greenhouse gases are warming the world. Over the last century, the planet has experienced the largest increase in surface temperature in 1,300 years. The average surface temperature of Earth rose 0.6 to 0.9°C (1.08°F to 1.62°F) between 1906 and 2006, and the rate of temperature increase nearly doubled in the last 50 years. Worldwide measurements of sea level show a rise of about 0.17 m (0.56 ft.) during the 20th century. The world's glaciers have steadily receded, and Arctic sea ice extent has steadily shrunk by 2.7% per decade since 1978.

Even if greenhouse gas concentrations stabilized today, the planet would continue to warm by about 0.6°C over the next century because it takes years for Earth to fully react to increases in greenhouse gases. As Earth has warmed, much of the excess energy has gone into heating the upper layers of the ocean. Scientists suspect that currents have transported some of this excess heat from surface waters down deep, removing it from the surface of our planet. Once the lower layers of the ocean have warmed, the excess heat in the upper layers will no longer be drawn down, and Earth will warm about 0.6°C (1°F).

But, how do scientists know global warming is caused by humans and that the observed warming isn't a natural variation in Earth's climate? Scientists use three closely connected methods to understand changes in Earth's climate. They look at records of Earth's past climates to see how and why climate changed in the past, they build computer models that allow them to see how the climate works, and they closely monitor Earth's current vital signs with an array of instruments ranging from space-based satellites to deep-sea thermometers. Records of past climate change reveal the natural events—such as volcanic eruptions and solar activity—that influenced climate throughout Earth's history. Today, scientists monitor those same natural events, as well as human-released greenhouse gases, and use computer models to determine how each influences Earth's climate.

Reconstructing Past Climate Change

Like detectives at a crime scene, scientists reconstruct past climate changes by looking for evidence left in things like glacial ice, ocean sediments, rocks, and trees. For example, glacial ice traps tiny samples of Earth's atmosphere, giving scientists a record of greenhouse gases that stretches back more than 650,000 years, and the chemical makeup of the ice provides clues to the average global temperature. From these and other records, scientists have built a record of Earth's past climates, or "paleoclimates." Paleoclimatology allowed scientists to show that climate changes in the past have been triggered by variations in Earth's orbit, solar variation, volcanic eruptions, and greenhouse gases.

Building a Climate Model

Next, to understand how sunlight, air, water, and land come together to create Earth's climate, scientists build climate models—computer simulations of the climate system. Climate models include the fundamental laws of physics—conservation of energy, mass, and momentum—as well as dozens of factors that influence Earth's climate. Though the models are complicated, rigorous tests with real-world data hone them into robust tools that allow scientists to experiment with the climate in a way not otherwise possible. For example, when scientists at NASA's Goddard Institute for Space Studies (GISS), NASA's division spearheading climate modeling efforts, put measurements of volcanic particles from Mount Pinatubo's 1991 eruption into their climate models well after the event, the models reported that Earth would have cooled by around 0.5°C a year or so later. The prediction matched cooling that had been observed around the globe after the eruption.

As the models reconstruct events that match the climate record, researchers gain confidence that the models are accurately duplicating the complex interactions that drive Earth's climate. Scientists then experiment with the models to gain insight into what is driving climate change. By experimenting with the models—removing greenhouse gases emitted by the burning of fossil fuels or changing the intensity of the Sun to see how each influences the climate—scientists can use the models to explain Earth's current climate and predict its future climate. So far, the only way scientists can get the models to match the rise in temperature seen over the past century is to include the greenhouse gases that humans have put into the atmosphere. This means that, according to the models, humans are responsible for most of the warming observed during the second half of the 20th century.

But, why do scientists trust results from climate models when models seem to have so much trouble forecasting the weather? It turns out that trends are easier to predict than specific events. Weather is a short-term, small-scale set of measurements of environmental conditions, while climate is the average of those conditions over a large area for a long time. The difference between predicting weather and climate is similar to the difference between predicting when a particular person will die versus calculating the average life span of an entire population. Given the large number of variables that influence conditions in Earth's lower atmosphere, and given that chaos also plays a larger role on shorter and smaller scales of time and space, weather is much harder to predict than the averages that make up climate.

However, the longer the timescale, the harder it becomes to predict climate. Scientists understand how certain processes that drive Earth's climate work now, and so they can accurately predict how events like Pinatubo's eruption will cool the globe's average temperature. But, they don't understand how every aspect of the climate system will change as the planet warms. Feedback loops—in which change in one part of the climate system produces change in another part—make climate harder to forecast as scientists look farther into the future. For example, what will happen to clouds as Earth warms? Will high-flying, heat-absorbing clouds that would cause additional heating become more frequent than dense, sunlight-blocking clouds? Will changes be regional or global, and how will they affect global climate? As of now, scientists can't answer these questions, and the uncertainties mean that global climate models provide a range of predictions instead of a highly detailed forecast.

Observing Global Warming

Climate models and paleoclimate information tell scientists what kinds of symptoms to look for when diagnosing global warming. Ocean temperatures and acidity should rise as the oceans soak up more heat and carbon dioxide. Global temperatures are predicted to increase, with the largest temperature increases over land and at the poles. Glaciers and sea ice will melt and sea levels will rise. Like a patient in a hospital, Earth is closely monitored for these symptoms by a fleet of satellites and surface instruments. NASA satellites record a host of vital signs, including atmospheric aerosols (particles from things like factories, fires, or erupting volcanoes), atmospheric gases, energy from Earth's surface and the Sun, ocean surface temperatures, global sea levels, the extent of ice sheets, glaciers and sea ice, plant growth, rainfall, cloud structure, and more. On the ground, networks of weather stations maintain temperature and rainfall records, and buoys measure deep ocean temperatures.

Along with paleoclimate data, these sources reveal that the planet has been warming for at least the last 400 years, and possibly the last 1,000 years. As of now, warming after 1950 cannot be explained without accounting for greenhouse gases; natural influences such as volcanic eruptions or changes in the Sun's output cannot account for the observed temperature changes.

Occasional violent volcanic eruptions, such as Mount Pinatubo, pump gases like sulfur dioxide and aerosols high into the atmosphere where they can linger for more than a year, reflecting sunlight and shading Earth's surface. The cooling influence of this aerosol "shade" is greater than the warming influence of the volcanoes' greenhouse gas emissions, and, therefore, such eruptions cannot account for the recent warming trend.

An increase in solar output also falls short of explaining recent warming. NASA satellites have been measuring the Sun's output since 1978, and while the Sun's activity has varied a little, the observed changes were not large enough to account for the warming recorded during the same period. Climate simulations of global temperature changes based only on solar variability and volcanic aerosols since 1750—omitting greenhouse gases—are able to fit the record of global temperatures only up until about 1950.

The only viable explanation for warming after 1950 is an increase in greenhouse gases. It is well established theoretically why carbon dioxide, methane, and other greenhouse gases should heat the planet, and observations show that they have.

Predicting Future Warming

As the world consumes ever more fossil fuel energy, greenhouse gas concentrations will continue to rise, and Earth's average surface temperature will rise with them. Based on plausible emission scenarios, the IPCC estimates that average surface temperatures could rise between 2°C and 6°C by the end of the 21st century.

At first glance, these numbers probably do not seem threatening. After all, temperatures typically change a few tens of degrees whenever a storm front moves through. Such temperature changes, however, represent day-to-day regional fluctuations. When surface temperatures are averaged over the entire globe for extended periods of time, it turns out that the average is remarkably stable. Not since the end of the last ice age 20,000 years ago, when Earth warmed about 5°C, has the average surface temperature changed as dramatically as the 2°C to 6°C change that scientists are predicting for the next century.

Scientists predict the range of temperature increase by running different scenarios through climate models. Because scientists can't say how human society may change over the next century, or how certain aspects of the climate system (such as clouds) will respond to global warming, they give a range of temperature estimates. The higher estimates are made on the assumption that the entire world will continue to use more and more fossil fuel per capita. The lower estimates come from best-case scenarios in which environmentally friendly technologies such as fuel cells and solar panels replace much of today's fossil fuel combustion. After inputting estimates for future greenhouse gas emissions, scientists run the models forward into many possible futures to arrive at the range of estimates provided in the IPCC report. The estimates are being used to predict how rising temperatures will affect both people and natural ecosystems. The severity of environmental change will depend on how much the Earth's surface warms over the next century.

Potential Effects of Global Warming

The most obvious impact of global warming will be changes in both average and extreme temperature and precipitation, but warming will also enhance coastal erosion, lengthen the growing season, melt ice caps and glaciers, and alter the range of some infectious diseases, among other things.

For most places, global warming will result in more hot days and fewer cool days, with the greatest warming happening over land. Longer, more intense heat waves will become more frequent. High latitudes and generally wet places will tend to receive more rainfall, while tropical regions and generally dry places will probably receive less rain. Increases in rainfall will come in the form of bigger, wetter storms, rather than in the form of more rainy days. In between those larger storms will be longer periods of light or no rain, so the frequency of drought will increase. Hurricanes will likely increase in intensity due to warmer ocean surface temperatures.

It is impossible to pin any one unusual weather event on global warming, but evidence is emerging that suggests that global warming is already influencing the weather. The IPCC reports that both heat waves and intense rain events have increased in frequency during the last 50 years, and human-induced global warming more likely than not contributed to the trend. Satellite-based rainfall measurements show tropical areas got more rain in the form of large storms or light rainfall instead of moderate storms between 1979 and 2003. Since the 1970s, the area affected by drought and the number of intense tropical cyclones also have increased, trends that IPCC scientists say were more likely than not influenced by human activities, though in the case of cyclones, the record is too sparse to draw any certain conclusions.

The weather isn't the only thing global warming will impact: rising sea levels will erode coasts and cause more frequent coastal flooding. The problem is serious because as much as 10% of the world's population lives in coastal areas less than 10 m (about 30 ft.) above sea level. The IPCC estimates that sea levels will rise between 0.18 and 0.59 m (0.59–1.9 ft.) by 2099 because of expanding sea water and melting mountain glaciers.

These estimates of sea level rise may be low, however, because they do not account for changes in the rate of melt from the world's major ice sheets. As temperatures rise, ice will melt more quickly. New satellite measurements reveal that the Greenland and West Antarctic ice sheets are shedding about 125 billion tons of ice per year—enough to raise sea levels by 0.35 mm (0.01 in.) per year. If the melting were to accelerate, the rise in sea level could be significantly higher. For instance, the last time global temperatures were a degree or so warmer than today, sea levels were about 6 m (20 ft.) higher, with the water mainly coming from the melting of the Greenland and the West Antarctic ice sheets. Neither ice sheet is likely to disappear before 2100, but there is the danger that global warming could initiate massive losses from the Greenland and Antarctic ice sheets that will continue or even accelerate over future centuries.

Global warming is also putting pressure on ecosystems, the plants and animals that coexist in a particular climate. Warmer temperatures have already shifted the growing season in many parts of the globe. Spring is coming earlier, and that means that migrating animals have to start earlier to follow food sources. And, since the growing season is longer, plants need more water to keep growing or they will dry out, increasing the risk of fires. Shorter, milder winters fail to kill insects, increasing the risk that an infestation will destroy an ecosystem. As the growing season progresses, maximum daily temperatures increase, sometimes beyond the tolerance of the plant or animal. To survive the climbing temperatures, both marine and land-based plants and animals have started to migrate toward the poles. Those species that cannot migrate or adapt face extinction. The IPCC estimates that 20–30% of plant and animal species will be at risk of extinction if temperatures climb more than 1.5°C to 2.5°C.

The people who will be hardest hit will be residents of poorer countries who do not have the resources to fend off changes in climate. As tropical temperature zones expand, the reach of some infectious diseases like malaria will change. More intense rains and hurricanes, rising sea levels, and fast-melting mountain glaciers will lead to more severe flooding. Hotter summers and more frequent fires will lead to more cases of heatstroke and deaths, and to higher levels of near-surface ozone and smoke, which would cause more "code red" air quality days. Intense droughts could lead to an increase in malnutrition. On a longer timescale, freshwater will become scarcer during the summer as mountain glaciers disappear, particularly in Asia and parts of North America. On the flip side, warmer winters will lead to fewer cold-related deaths, and the longer growing season could increase food production in some temperate areas.

Ultimately, global warming will impact life on Earth in many ways, but the extent of the change is up to us. Scientists have shown that human emissions of greenhouse gases are pushing global temperatures up, and many aspects of climate are responding to the warming in the way that scientists predicted they would. Ecosystems across the globe are already affected and surprising changes have already taken place. Polar ice caps are melting, plants and animals are migrating, tropical rain is shifting, and droughts are becoming more widespread and frequent. Since greenhouse gases are long-lived, the planet will continue to warm and changes will continue to happen, but the degree to which global warming changes life on Earth depends on our decisions.

Reprinted from *Earth Observatory* (May 11, 2007), courtesy of NASA.

The Water Cycle

Viewed from space, one of the most striking features of our home planet is the water, in both liquid and frozen forms, that covers approximately 75% of Earth's surface. Geologic evidence suggests that large amounts of water have likely flowed on Earth for the past 3.8 billion years—most of its existence. Believed to have initially arrived on the surface through the emissions of ancient volcanoes, water is a vital substance that sets Earth apart from the rest of the planets in our solar system. In particular, water appears to be a necessary ingredient for the development and nourishment of life.

Water, Water, Everywhere

Water is practically everywhere on Earth. Moreover, it is the only known substance that can naturally exist as a gas, a liquid, and a solid within the relatively small range of air temperatures and pressures found at Earth's surface.

In all, Earth's water content is about 1.39 billion km^3 (331 million $mi.^3$), with the bulk of it, about 96.5%, being in the global oceans. As for the rest, approximately 1.7% is stored in the polar ice caps, glaciers, and permanent snow, and another 1.7% is stored in groundwater, lakes, rivers, streams, and soil. Only one-thousandth of 1% of the water on Earth exists as water vapor in the atmosphere.

Despite its small amount, this water vapor has a huge influence on the planet. Water vapor is a powerful greenhouse gas, and it is a major driver of the Earth's weather and climate as it travels around the globe, transporting latent heat with it. Latent heat is heat obtained by water molecules as they transition from liquid or solid to vapor; the heat is released when the molecules condense from vapor back to liquid or solid form, creating cloud droplets and various forms of precipitation.

For human needs, the amount of freshwater on Earth—for drinking and agriculture—is particularly important. Freshwater exists in lakes, rivers, groundwater, and frozen as snow and ice. Estimates of groundwater are particularly difficult to make, and they vary widely.

Groundwater may constitute anywhere from approximately 22 to 30% of freshwater, with ice (including ice caps, glaciers, permanent snow, ground ice, and permafrost) accounting for most of the remaining 78 to 70%.

A Multiphased Journey

The water, or hydrologic, cycle describes the pilgrimage of water as water molecules make their way from Earth's surface to the atmosphere and back again, and in some cases to below the surface. This gigantic system, powered by energy from the Sun, is a continuous exchange of moisture between the oceans, the atmosphere, and the land.

Studies have revealed that evaporation—the process by which water changes from a liquid to a gas—from oceans, seas, and other bodies of water (lakes, rivers, streams) provides nearly 90% of the moisture in our atmosphere. Most of the remaining 10%

found in the atmosphere is released by plants through transpiration. Plants take in water through their roots, and then release it through small pores on the underside of their leaves. In addition, a very small portion of water vapor enters the atmosphere through sublimation, the process by which water changes directly from a solid (ice or snow) to a gas. The gradual shrinking of snow banks in cases when the temperature remains below freezing results from sublimation.

Together, evaporation, transpiration, and sublimation, plus volcanic emissions, account for almost all the water vapor in the atmosphere that is not inserted through human activities. While evaporation from the oceans is the primary vehicle for driving the surface-to-atmosphere portion of the hydrologic cycle, transpiration is also significant. For example, a cornfield 1 acre in size can transpire as much as 4,000 gallons of water every day.

After the water enters the lower atmosphere, rising air currents carry it upward, often high into the atmosphere, where the air is cooler. In the cool air, water vapor is more likely to condense from a gas to a liquid to form cloud droplets. Cloud droplets can grow and produce precipitation (including rain, snow, sleet, freezing rain, and hail), which is the primary mechanism for transporting water from the atmosphere back to Earth's surface.

When precipitation falls over the land surface, it follows various routes in its subsequent paths. Some of it evaporates, returning to the atmosphere; some seeps into the ground as soil moisture or groundwater; and some runs off into rivers and streams. Almost all of the water eventually flows into the oceans or other bodies of water, where the cycle continues. At different stages of the cycle, some of the water is intercepted by humans or other life forms for drinking, washing, irrigating, and a large variety of other uses.

Groundwater is found in two broadly defined layers of the soil, the "zone of aeration," where gaps in the soil are filled with both air and water, and, further down, the "zone of saturation," where the gaps are completely filled with water. The boundary between these two zones is known as the *water table*, which rises or falls as the amount of groundwater changes.

The amount of water in the atmosphere at any moment in time is only 12,900 km³, a minute fraction of Earth's total water supply; if it were to completely rain out, atmospheric moisture would cover Earth's surface to a depth of only 2.5 cm. However, far more water—in fact, some 495,000 km³ of it—is cycled through the atmosphere every year. It is as if the entire amount of water in the air were removed and replenished nearly 40 times a year.

Water continually evaporates, condenses, and precipitates, and on a global basis, evaporation approximately equals precipitation. Because of this equality, the total amount of water vapor in the atmosphere remains approximately the same over time. However, over the continents, precipitation routinely exceeds evaporation, and conversely, over the oceans, evaporation exceeds precipitation.

In the case of the oceans, the continual excess of evaporation versus precipitation would eventually leave the oceans empty if they were not being replenished by additional means. Not only are they being replenished, largely through runoff from the land areas, but over the past 100 years, they have been over-replenished: Sea level around the globe has risen approximately 17 cm over the course of the 20th century.

Sea level has risen both because of warming of the oceans, causing water to expand and increase in volume, and because more water has been entering the ocean than the amount leaving it through evaporation or other means. A primary cause for an increased mass of water entering the ocean is the calving or melting of land ice (ice sheets and glaciers). Sea ice is already in the ocean, so increases or decreases in the annual amount of sea ice do not significantly affect sea level.

Throughout the hydrologic cycle, there are many paths that a water molecule might follow. Water at the bottom of Lake Superior may eventually rise into the atmosphere and fall as rain in Massachusetts. Runoff from the Massachusetts rain may drain into the Atlantic Ocean and circulate north-eastward toward Iceland, destined to become part of a floe of sea ice, or, after evaporation to the atmosphere and precipitation as snow, part of a glacier.

Water molecules can take an immense variety of routes and branching trails that lead them again and again through the three phases of ice, liquid water, and water vapor. For instance, the water molecules that once fell 100 years ago as rain on your great-grandparents' farmhouse in Iowa might now be falling as snow on your driveway in California.

The Water Cycle and Climate Change

Among the most serious Earth science and environmental policy issues confronting society are the potential changes in the Earth's water cycle due to climate change. The science community now generally agrees that the Earth's climate is undergoing changes in response to natural variability, including solar variability, and increasing concentrations of greenhouse gases and aerosols. Furthermore, agreement is widespread that these changes may profoundly affect atmospheric water vapor concentrations, clouds, precipitation patterns, and runoff and stream-flow patterns.

For example, as the lower atmosphere becomes warmer, evaporation rates will increase, resulting in an increase in the amount of moisture circulating throughout the troposphere (lower atmosphere). An observed consequence of higher water vapor concentrations is the increased frequency of intense precipitation events, mainly over land areas. Furthermore, because of warmer temperatures, more precipitation is falling as rain rather than snow.

In parts of the Northern Hemisphere, an earlier arrival of springlike conditions is leading to earlier peaks in snowmelt and resulting river flows. As a consequence, seasons with the highest water demand, typically summer and fall, are being impacted by a reduced availability of freshwater.

Warmer temperatures have led to increased drying of the land surface in some areas, with the effect of an increased incidence and severity of drought. The Palmer Drought Severity Index is a measure of soil moisture using precipitation measurements and rough estimates of changes in evaporation. This index has shown that from 1900 to 2002, the Sahel region of Africa has been experiencing harsher drought conditions. This same index also indicates an opposite trend in southern South America and the south-central United States.

While the brief scenarios described above represent a small portion of the observed changes in the water cycle, it should be noted that many uncertainties remain in the prediction of future climate. These uncertainties derive from the sheer complexity of the climate system, insufficient and incomplete data sets, and inconsistent results given by current climate models. However, state-of-the-art (but still incomplete and imperfect) climate models do consistently predict that precipitation will become more variable, with increased risks of drought and floods at different times and places.

Observing the Water Cycle

Orbiting satellites are now collecting data relevant to all aspects of the hydrologic cycle, including evaporation, transpiration, condensation, precipitation, and runoff. The National Aeronautics and Space Administration (NASA) even has one satellite, *Aqua*, named specifically for the information it is collecting about the many components of the water cycle.

Aqua launched on May 4, 2002, with six Earth-observing instruments: the Atmospheric Infrared Sounder (AIRS), the Advanced Microwave Sounding Unit (AMSU), the Humidity Sounder for Brazil (HSB), the Advanced Microwave Scanning Radiometer for the Earth Observing System (AMSR-E), the Moderate Resolution Imaging Spectroradiometer (MODIS), and Clouds and the Earth's Radiant Energy System (CERES).

Since water vapor is Earth's primary greenhouse gas, and it contributes significantly to uncertainties in projections of future global warming, it is critical to understand how it varies in the Earth system. In the first years of the *Aqua* mission, AIRS, AMSU, and HSB provided space-based measurements of atmospheric temperature and water vapor that were more accurate than any obtained before; the sensors also made measurements from more altitudes than any previous sensor. The HSB is no longer operational, but the AIRS/AMSU system continues to provide high-quality atmospheric temperature and water vapor measurements.

More recent studies using AIRS data have demonstrated that most of the warming caused by carbon dioxide does not come directly from carbon dioxide, but rather from increased water vapor and other factors that amplify the initial warming. Other studies have shown improved estimation of the landfall of a hurricane in the Bay of Bengal by incorporating AIRS temperature measurements, and improved understanding of large-scale atmospheric patterns such as the Madden-Julian Oscillation.

In addition to their importance to our weather, clouds play a major role in regulating Earth's climate system. MODIS, CERES, and AIRS all collect data relevant to the study of clouds. The cloud data include the height and area of clouds, the liquid water they contain, and the sizes of cloud droplets and ice particles. The size of cloud particles affects how they reflect and absorb incoming sunlight, and the reflectivity (albedo) of clouds plays a major role in Earth's energy balance.

One of the many variables AMSR-E monitors is global precipitation. The sensor measures microwave energy, some of which passes through clouds, and so the sensor can detect the rainfall even under the clouds.

Water in the atmosphere is hardly the only focus of the *Aqua* mission. Among much else, AMSR-E and MODIS are being used to study sea ice. Sea ice is important to the Earth system, not just as an important element in the habitat of polar bears, penguins, and some species of seals. Sea ice also can insulate the underlying liquid water against heat loss to the often frigid overlying polar atmosphere, and it reflects sunlight that would otherwise be available to warm the ocean.

When it comes to sea ice, AMSR-E and MODIS provide complementary information. AMSR-E does not record as much detail about ice features as MODIS does, but it can distinguish ice versus open water even when it is cloudy. The AMSR-E measurements continue, with improved resolution and accuracy, a satellite record of changes in the extent of polar ice that extends back to the 1970s.

AMSR-E and MODIS also provide monitoring of snow coverage over land, another key indicator of climate change. As with sea ice, AMSR-E allows routine monitoring of the snow, irrespective of cloud cover, but with less spatial detail, while MODIS sees greater spatial detail, but only under cloud-free conditions.

As for liquid water on land, AMSR-E provides information about soil moisture, which is crucial for vegetation including agricultural crops. AMSR-E's monitoring of soil moisture globally permits, for example, the early identification of signs of drought.

More Water Cycle Observations

Aqua is the most comprehensive of NASA's water cycle missions, but it is not alone. In fact, the Terra satellite also has MODIS and CERES instruments onboard, and several other spacecraft have made or are making unique water-cycle measurements.

The Ice, Cloud, and Land Elevation Satellite (ICESat) was launched in January 2003. It collected data on the topography of Earth's ice sheets, clouds, vegetation, and the thickness of sea ice off and on until October 2009. A new ICESat mission, ICESat-2, is now under development and is scheduled to launch in 2015.

The Gravity Recovery and Climate Experiment (GRACE) is a unique mission that consists of two spacecraft orbiting one behind the other; changes in the distance between the two provide information about the gravity field on Earth below. Because gravity depends on mass, some of the changes in gravity over time signal a shift in water from one place on Earth to another. Through measurements of changing gravity fields, GRACE scientists are able to derive information about changes in the mass of ice sheets and glaciers and even changes in groundwater around the world.

CloudSat is advancing scientists' understanding of cloud abundance, distribution, structure, and radiative properties (how they absorb and emit energy, including thermal infrared energy escaping from Earth's surface).

Since 2006, *CloudSat* has flown the first satellite-based, millimeter-wavelength cloud radar—an instrument that is 1,000 times more sensitive than existing weather radars on the ground. Unlike ground-based weather radars that use centimeter wavelengths to detect raindrop-sized particles, *CloudSat*'s radar allows the detection of the much smaller particles of liquid water and ice in the large cloud masses that contribute significantly to our weather.

The joint NASA and French Cloud-Aerosol Lidar and Infrared Pathfinder Satellite Observations (CALIPSO) is providing new insight into the role that clouds and atmospheric aerosols (particles like dust and pollution) play in regulating Earth's weather, climate, and air quality. CALIPSO combines an active laser instrument with passive infrared and visible imagers to probe the vertical structure and properties of thin clouds and aerosols over the globe.

Reprinted from *Earth Observatory* (September 22, 2007), courtesy of NASA.

The Greenhouse Effect

Earth's distance from the Sun has been influential in determining its climate. If Earth were much closer to the Sun, it might resemble Venus. Venus is described as a "hellish" place because the atmosphere filters out most of the visible spectrum of light but red. The second planet from the Sun, located between Mercury and Earth, Venus has an atmosphere that is 96% carbon dioxide (CO_2). Earth's atmosphere is only 0.035% CO_2. The CO_2 layer on Venus is so thick that it holds in almost all of the heat absorbed from the Sun, allowing little to escape—a phenomenon known as the greenhouse effect. As a result, the average temperature on Venus is 457°C, far too hot for any life as we know it to exist.

Earth exhibits a slight greenhouse effect, too, but obviously not to the degree that Venus does. The greenhouse effect is life-sustaining, up to a point. Without it, the average temperature on Earth would be much lower, perhaps too cold for life to exist. At present, the greenhouse effect here is beneficial, but it may not always be so. The greenhouse effect on Earth is primarily due to water vapor in the atmosphere; however, CO_2 also contributes to the effect, and it is this greenhouse gas that is causing the greatest concern at present. CO_2 is a by-product of many things that we do, primarily the burning of fossil fuels—coal, oil, and gasoline. As more and more CO_2 is added to the atmosphere, the greenhouse effect increases, but it is unclear what the impact on climate will be because of many intervening factors.

Made of glass or translucent plastic, the climate-controlled greenhouse is perfect for nurseries to grow seedling plants and flowers. The glass walls and roof permit the plants to get the most sunlight possible. But, the glass also traps heat in the greenhouse. *Greenhouse effect* is the name given to this phenomenon when substances, like glass, allow sunlight to pass through them but do not allow radiant heat to escape. Any time you have entered a car that has been sitting in the sun with the windows rolled up, you have experienced the greenhouse effect.

The greenhouse effect exists because of the nature of light. Some forms of light are visible (like the colors in the rainbow) but others, like radiant heat (also called infrared radiation), are invisible. The greenhouse effect involves both visible and invisible light. The beginning of the process can be explained with a common example.

Paved roads can become extremely hot in the sunlight. Two different kinds of light come into play in heating the pavement. The light from the Sun strikes the pavement in the form of visible light. As the pavement absorbs this light, it heats up and then gives off heat. The temperature of the pavement will continue to rise until the amount of radiant heat (energy released to the environment as heat) given off is equal to the amount of energy absorbed from the sunlight. In direct sunlight, the resulting pavement temperature can be quite high, as anyone crossing an asphalt street barefoot on a summer day can testify.

The same principle operates in the greenhouse effect. The visible light from the Sun passes unimpeded through the glass of a greenhouse and strikes everything—the plants, the tables, the floor. These objects absorb the light and their temperatures increase. The objects then begin to radiate heat in the form of infrared light. However, the glass will not permit the infrared light (heat) to pass through it and escape, so all the heat stays trapped in the greenhouse.

Although CO_2 accounts for a tiny percentage of Earth's atmosphere (much less than 1%), it acts like the glass of a greenhouse, allowing sunlight to pass through and heat Earth, but partially preventing the resulting radiant heat from escaping out into space. Some of the radiant heat is reflected or absorbed by the CO_2 molecules, heating the lower atmosphere. Fortunately, the CO_2 content is not high enough to trap all of the infrared light, but since the start of the Industrial Revolution, more CO_2 is being produced every day as people burn coal, oil, and gas. Earth has natural processes that remove CO_2 from the atmosphere—photosynthesis and incorporation into ocean sediments—but they may not keep pace. We are in danger of warming up the planet and that presents serious consequences. Weather patterns could change and cropland could become unsuitable for farming. Melting polar ice caps could cause sea levels to rise and coastlines to flood.

The Coming Climate Crisis?

Dr. Claire L. Parkinson has been a climate scientist at NASA's Goddard Space Flight Center in Greenbelt, Maryland, since 1978 and has been the project scientist for the *Aqua* mission since 1993. She is the author of a book about what many fear to be a "coming climate crisis." In the book, Dr. Parkinson summarizes the 4.6 billion years of climate change on Earth and points out that there have been periods when Earth was much warmer than it is now and also periods when Earth was much cooler than it is now.

Dr. Parkinson includes a brief history of human impacts on climate and discusses predictions about what may happen in the future. Some of these predictions are quite bleak, but not all scientists agree with the predictions. She cautions that there are limitations to the computer models we use to predict future climate, but that still it appears that the basic conclusion of expected increased warming is most likely correct. This conclusion is based on the fact that humans are significantly increasing the concentration of greenhouse gases in the atmosphere. These gases allow the Sun's radiation to come through the atmosphere fairly readily but hinder Earth's radiation from getting out. Humans also are doing other things that instead have a cooling effect, but the predominance of the evidence shows that the warming from increased greenhouse gases is dominating and likely will continue to dominate for some time.

However, despite the legitimate concern about global warming, Parkinson cautions against jumping on the geoengineering bandwagon of trying to intentionally modify future climate as a solution to the concern about excessive warming. Quite a few schemes to cool the planet through the use of various engineering technologies (hence the term *geoengineering*) have been proposed. One large category of these would be to reflect sunlight away from Earth, with the reflection coming alternatively outside of Earth's atmosphere, within Earth's atmosphere, or at Earth's surface. Another category is to reduce the carbon dioxide—an important greenhouse gas—in the atmosphere, either by capturing it at emission sources or by taking it out of the atmosphere.

Parkinson considers several of these geoengineering schemes and warns that massive geoengineering "could backfire and become a greater disaster than the one we are trying to correct." Among the problems, for instance, would be the damage to ecosystems if reflective surfaces were placed over large areas of deserts or oceans, as has been proposed, or the damage to weather patterns, the ozone layer, and perhaps human health if massive amounts of particulate matter were poured into the upper atmosphere, as has also been proposed, the intent being to reflect away sunlight. Alternatives to geoengineering could include the safe reduction in human-induced emissions to the atmosphere and oceans. Parkinson includes a separate chapter on various ways of doing that.

Parkinson's research program has been largely centered on satellite data analysis of sea ice and its role in the global climate system. She is also involved in climate modeling and satellite imagery and has done fieldwork in both the Arctic and Antarctic, including as chief scientist on an expedition to Resolute Bay and the North Pole in April 1999. Parkinson has written a book on satellite imagery and a history of Western science, and she has coauthored atlases of sea ice and a textbook on climate modeling.

Reasons for the Seasons

The reason why Earth has four seasons—spring, summer, fall, winter—is often misunderstood. In part, this misunderstanding comes from diagrams similar to **Figure R12.1** where we try to give you a perspective on a nearly circular orbit as it would appear to a viewer almost in the plane of the orbit. From this perspective, the circular orbit looks elliptical. A similar perspective from directly above Earth's nearly circular orbit around the Sun looks like the diagram in **Figure R12.2**. Having learned that Earth's orbit is actually an ellipse (although the ellipse is so round it is almost a circle), many people jump to the conclusion that diagrams like **Figure R12.1** represent the actual orbit around the Sun rather than a perspective view. This incorrect interpretation of the diagram then causes people to think that the planet is hotter in the summer because Earth is closer to the Sun than in the winter. Consider the following example. At the exact same time it is summer in the United States (the Northern Hemisphere), it is winter in Australia (the Southern Hemisphere). If Earth's distance from the Sun determines the seasons, then it should be the same season everywhere on the planet. In fact, Earth is actually farther away from the Sun during our (the Northern Hemisphere's) summer than it is during our winter.

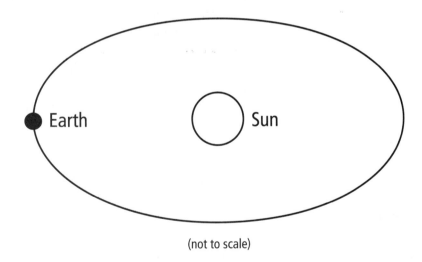

(not to scale)

Figure R12.1 Earth's orbit around the Sun is not the extreme ellipse shown here.

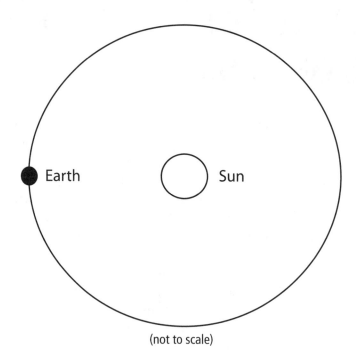

Figure R12.2
Earth's circular orbit
around the Sun

(not to scale)

Earth's orbit around the Sun is more accurately represented by the circle drawn in **Figure R12.2**. This slightly elliptical orbit does not account for the seasons, but another of Earth's characteristics of motion does.

Earth is spinning. When a ball spins, the line around which the ball turns is called the axis of rotation. Earth's axis of rotation is tilted in relation to the plane of Earth's orbit around the Sun. **Figure R12.3** illustrates the difference. As Earth is spinning, it is also moving around the Sun. The position of Earth in its orbit around the Sun, combined with the tilt of the axis of rotation, then determines the season. **Figure R12.4** and **Figure R12.5** show how the orbit and axis tilt work together. In the summer, the Sun's rays are striking at as close to a 90° angle to the surface as is possible for that location.

Austin, Texas, is located at latitude 30° and Minneapolis, Minnesota, is located at latitude 45°. On the longest day of the year, called the summer solstice, the Sun's rays strike Austin at 83.5° at noon and strike Minneapolis at 68.5°. During this time of year, the Sun's radiation is most intense. **Figure R12.5** shows what happens six months later when Earth is on the other side of the Sun. On the shortest day of the year, the winter solstice, the Sun's rays strike Austin at an angle of 36.5° and strike Minneapolis at an angle of 21.5°. In this case, the Sun's rays are hitting the surface at a greater slant than they do during the summer, and the heating is not as efficient. It is not as efficient because the same amount of solar radiation is being spread out over a larger area. Compare **Figure R12.4** and **Figure R12.5**. The second figure represents our winter.

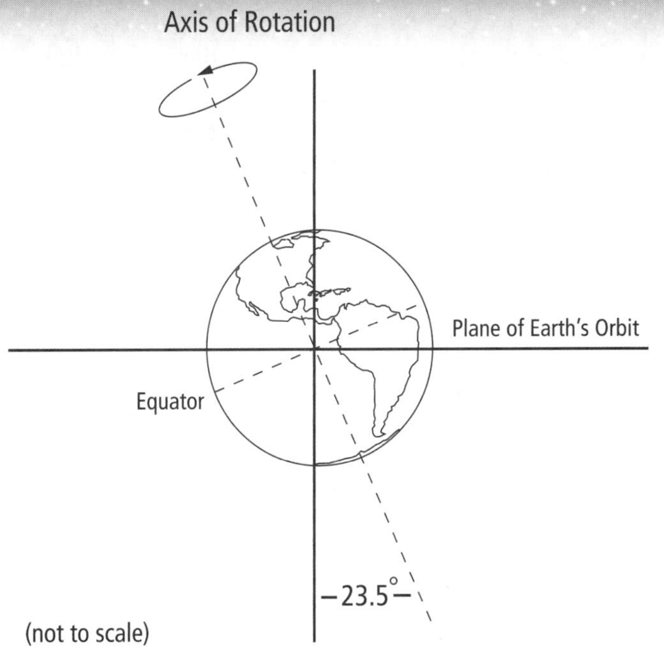

Axis of Rotation

Plane of Earth's Orbit

Equator

—23.5°—

(not to scale)

Figure R12.3
Tilt of Earth's axis

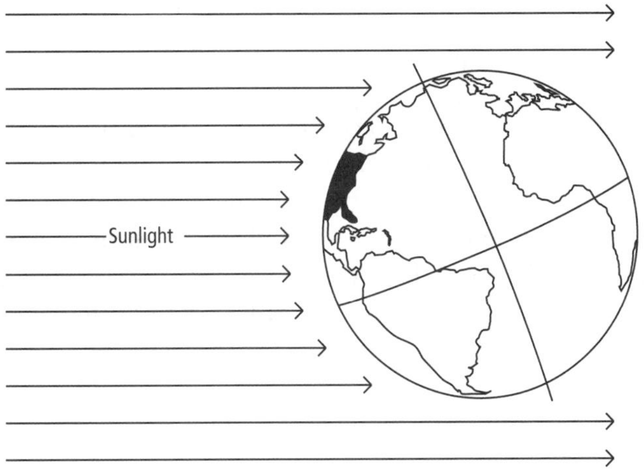

Sunlight

Figure R12.4
Summer in the Northern
Hemisphere

Sunlight

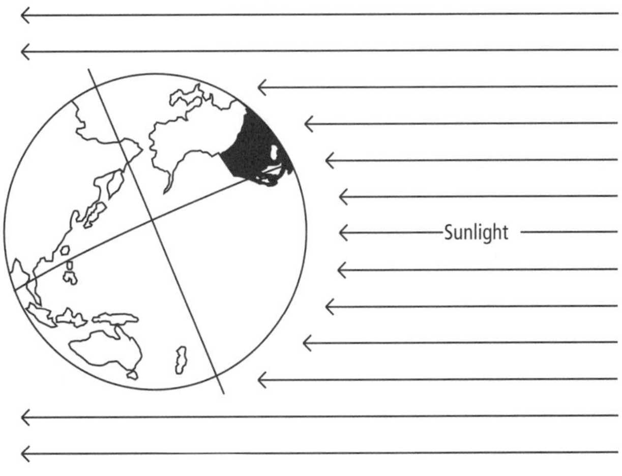

Figure R12.5
Winter in the Northern
Hemisphere

Figure R12.6 illustrates why perpendicular rays of light are more efficient at heating than slanting rays. In the picture at the top, the paper is standing vertically and the energy from the rays is concentrated in the small area (A_1). But, when the paper is tilted back, notice that the same number of light rays, hence the same amount of energy, is now spread over a much larger area (A_2); therefore, the paper will not heat as fast.

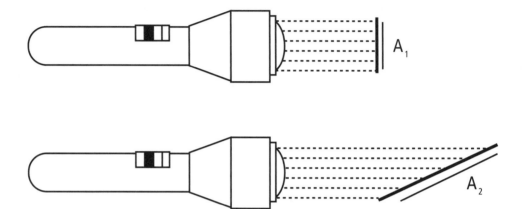

Figure R12.6
Perpendicular rays of light are more efficient at heating than slanting rays.

Similarly, when part of the surface of Earth is tilted with respect to the rays of sunlight, it will receive slanting solar rays and not heat as fast. Since Earth is round, some locations can be receiving direct sunlight while others receive it indirectly. This explains why it can be summer on one part of the planet and winter on another part. In addition, because of the axis tilt, the days in summer are longer (allowing more time for solar heating) than in winter.

Phases of the Moon

The Moon is the source of one of the most prevalent misconceptions in astronomy. The misconception is based on the belief that the Moon appears to change shape in a cyclical pattern every 29.5 days.

Throughout recorded history, people have been fascinated with the changing shape of the Moon. Every 29.5 days, the shape of the Moon predictably changes from a complete circle to a half circle to a crescent shape and then vanishes to rebuild again from a sliver of a crescent. Two common misconceptions attempt to explain the changing shape of the Moon. One is that clouds block our view of part of the Moon. The other is that the shadow of Earth falls on the Moon hiding different parts of it at different times. (The only time Earth's shadow falls on the Moon is during a lunar eclipse.)

In fact, the amount of the Moon that is illuminated is constant. We simply cannot see the entire illuminated portion all the time. When we can only see the shadowed ("dark") side of the Moon, it is referred to as the "new" Moon. To understand what is happening when we have a new Moon, imagine yourself in a totally dark room with a ball a couple of meters in front of you. In the dark, you would not be able to see the ball. Now, imagine that someone is standing in front of you on the other side of the ball and is shining a flashlight toward you. The light would shine on half the ball, but not the half you could see. You still would not be able to see the ball very well because the part facing you is shadowed (see **Figure R13.1**). This is like the new Moon.

New Moon

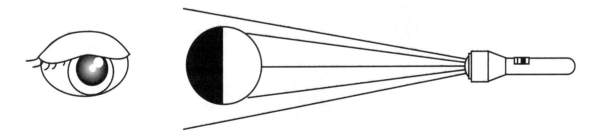

Figure R13.1 New Moon

Now, if *you* were to hold the light and shine it toward the ball, you would see the half that is illuminated. This is like the full Moon (see **Figure R13.2**). The illuminated part of the Moon as seen from Earth changes shape between a full Moon and new Moon because it is orbiting Earth. **Figure R13.3** shows the positions of Earth and the Moon relative to the incoming sunlight when the Moon is seen as "full" from Earth. Notice that the Moon appears to be above Earth. This is because the orbital plane of the Moon around Earth is tilted with respect to the plane of Earth's orbit around the Sun. If this were not so, there would be a lunar eclipse each month instead of only occasionally.

Full Moon

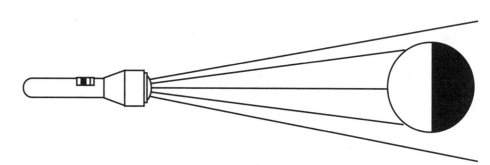

Figure R13.2
Full Moon

The shape of the full Moon and the new Moon are easy to explain. The other shapes—crescent, half Moon, gibbous—are more difficult, but each one relates to the path the Moon travels around Earth each month. A model for how these intermediate shapes can be visualized is shown in **Figure R13.4**. The inner ring of Moons shows that half of the Moon is always illuminated. The outer ring shows what can actually be seen from Earth.

Earth is the only planet in the solar system with one moon. Mercury and Venus have none, and Mars has two. The other planets have many moons.

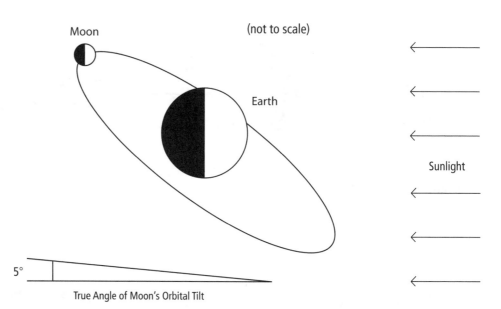

Figure R13.3
The tilted plane of the Moon's orbit

Note:
- Objects are not to scale.
- The inner circle shows a view from above Earth's North Pole.
- The outer circle is the view that we see from Earth.

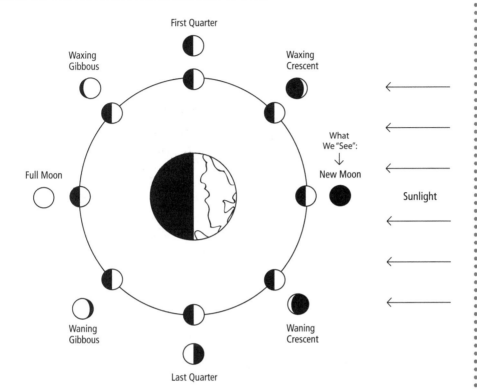

Figure R13.4
The phases of the Moon

Resources

This material was completely updated and revised by the authors for this new second edition. It is not meant to be a complete representation of resources in astronomy, but should assist teachers in further exploration of this subject. The entries are subdivided into the following categories:

- **Curricula and Activities**
  This category includes several curriculum-based activities from prominent, reliable astronomical sources such as the Lawrence Hall of Science at the University of California, Berkeley, and the Astronomical Society of the Pacific.

- **Software**
  This section lists a variety of software for astronomical simulations and star charts.

- **Websites**
  This category provides a wide variety of resources and activities on the latest astronomical research and data.

- **NASA Resources**
  The National Aeronautics and Space Administration (NASA) offers many educational resources for students and teachers on the subject of space. For example, the NASA Education website lists numerous educational resources available for students and teachers. NASA also has Educator Resource Centers.

Curricula and Activities

Great Explorations in Math and Science (GEMS)
Lawrence Hall of Science
University of California, Berkeley
Berkeley, CA 94720-5200
tel. 510-642-7771
fax 510-643-0309
e-mail: gems@berkeley.edu
www.lhs.berkeley.edu/gems

Educational resources include *Earth, Moon, and Stars; Invisible Universe; Living With a Star; Messages From Space; Moons of Jupiter; The Real Reasons for Seasons.*

PASS: Planetarium Activities for Student Success
Lawrence Hall of Science
University of California, Berkeley
Berkeley, CA 94720-5200
tel. 510-642-5132
e-mail: lhsweb@berkeley.edu
www.lhs.berkeley.edu/pass

Twelve volumes for grades K–12 on astronomy and space science.

FOSS: Full Option Science System
Lawrence Hall of Science
University of California, Berkeley
Berkeley, CA 94720-5200
tel. 510-642-5132
www.lhsfoss.org/index.html

FOSS is a research-based science program for grades K–8 developed at LHS with support from the National Science Foundation and published by Delta Education.

FOSS Middle School Course: *Earth and Space Science: Planetary Science*

Project ASTRO
Astronomical Society of the Pacific
390 Ashton Avenue
San Francisco, CA 94112
tel. 800-335-2624
www.astrosociety.org

ASP publishes *The Universe at Your Fingertips 2.0: A Collection of Hands-On, Classroom-Tested Activities and Resources for Teaching Astronomy* (DVD-ROM for grades 3–9).

Project STAR (Science Teaching Through Its Astronomical Roots): The Universe in Your Hands, 2001, 2nd edition
Kendall/Hunt Publishing Co.
4050 Westmark Drive
P.O. Box 1840
Dubuque, IA 52004
tel. 800-228-0810
Astronomy-based science course. Student textbook and teachers' resource with supporting materials. Produced by the Harvard-Smithsonian Center for Astrophysics (cfa-*www.Harvard.edu/cfa/sed*), grades 9–12.

Software

Starry Night software
www.starrynight.com

Starry Night Middle School is software with an accompanying curriculum.
www.starrynighteducation.com product_5-8.html
Interactive sky simulation (planetarium) software with lesson plans correlated to state and national standards.

Celestia
www.shatters.net/celestia/
Free sky simulation (planetarium) software.

Stellarium
www.stellarium.org
Free sky simulation (planetarium) software.

Websites

Space Telescope Science Institute (STScI)
3700 San Martin Drive
Baltimore, MD 21218
tel. 410-338-4700
www.stsci.edu

Amazing Space
amazing-space.stsci.edu
Web-based K–12 activities.

American Astronomical Society, Education Office
www.aas.org/education

Astronomical Society of the Pacific
www.astrosociety.org
Newsletter for teachers, magazine, posters, books, and other educational materials.

Astronomy Magazine
www.astronomy.com

Astronomy Picture of the Day
antwrp.gsfc.nasa.gov/apod/astropix.html

Bad Astronomy website
www.badastronomy.com
A popular website that debunks many myths about astronomy.

Careers in Astronomy
American Astronomical Society
www.aas.org/education/careers.phpl
http://members.aas.org/JobReg/JobRegister.cfm

Center for Educational Resources (CERES) Project
NASA & Montana State University
btc.montana.edu/ceres
Online library of K–12 astronomy resources.

Challenger Center for Space Science Education
www.challenger.org

Four Thousand Years of Women in Science
www.astr.ua.edu/4000WS

Good Astronomy Activities on the World Wide Web
Astronomical Society of the Pacific
www.astrosociety.org/education/activities/astroacts.html

Hands-On Universe Project (HOU)
Lawrence Hall of Science, University of California, Berkeley
www.handsonuniverse.org
A K–12 research and curriculum development program.

Hawaiian Astronomical Society
www.hawastsoc.org
Uses many up-to-date NASA pictures to illustrate concepts in introductory astronomy.

Heavens Above
www.heavens-above.com
Visible satellite passes and real-time orbit displays for any location in the world.

International Astronomical Union
www.iau.org

NASA Kids' Club
www.nasa.gov/audience/forkids/kidsclub/flash/index.html
Astronomy updates and background information on space.

National Optical Astronomy Observatory (NOAO) Educational & Public Outreach Program
www.noao.edu/education/noaoeo.html

Science Education Gateway (SEGway)
Center for Science Education, Space Sciences Laboratory, University of California, Berkeley
http://cse.ssl.berkeley.edu/segwayed/about.html
NASA scientists, science museums, and K–12 educators offer Earth and space science curricula via the World Wide Web.

The Space Place
NASA Jet Propulsion Laboratory, Pasadena, CA
http://spaceplace.nasa.gov/en/kids
Classroom activities, many for grades 9–12.

Sky and Telescope: The Essential Magazine of Astronomy
www.skyandtelescope.com

Skymaps
www.skymaps.com
Free printable star charts available each month.

The Why Files: The Science Behind the News
Graduate School of the University of Wisconsin-Madison
http://whyfiles.org
Explanations of the science behind the headlines.

Windows to the Universe
A website about the solar system in English and Spanish in three reading levels for both languages.
www.windows2universe.org

NASA Resources

The National Aeronautics and Space Administration (NASA) offers many educational resources for students and teachers on the subject of space. The NASA Education website—*www.nasa.gov/offices/education/programs/index.html*—lists numerous educational resources available for students and teachers for all grade levels from K–12 and higher. NASA also has Educator Resource Centers, listed below. Contact the center listed for your state.

NASA Education Websites

NASA Education
www.nasa.gov/offices/education/programs/index.html

NASA's Central Operation of Resources for Educators (CORE)
core.nasa.gov

The national distribution center for NASA's audiovisual educational materials.

NASA Science
http://science.nasa.gov

NASA Field Center Educator Resource Centers

Alaska, Northern California (southernmost counties of Inyo, Kings, Monterey, Tulare), Hawaii, Idaho, Montana, Nevada, Oregon, Utah, Washington, Wyoming
NASA Educator Resource Center
NASA Ames Research Center
Mail Stop 226-8
Moffett Field, CA 94035-1000
tel. 650-604-5544
fax 650-604-0978
http://amesnews.arc.nasa.gov/erc/erchome.html

Arizona, Southern California (northernmost counties of Kern, San Bernardino, San Luis Obispo)
NASA Educator Resource Center
NASA Dryden Flight Research Center
Office of Academic Investments
38256 Sierra Highway, Suite A
Palmdale, CA 93550
tel. 661-276-2445
fax 661-276-2010
www.dfrc.nasa.gov/Education/ERC/index.html

California
NASA Educator Resource Center
NASA Jet Propulsion Laboratory
Village at Indian Hill
1460 East Holt Avenue
Suite 20
Pomona, CA 91767
tel. 909-397-4420
fax 909-397-4470
http://learn.jpl.nasa.gov/resources/index.html

Illinois, Indiana, Michigan, Minnesota, Ohio, Wisconsin

NASA Educator Resource Center
NASA Glenn Research Center
21000 Brookpark Road, MS 8-1
Cleveland, OH 44135
tel. 216-433-2017
fax 216-433-3601
www.grc.nasa.gov/WWW/OEP/ERCN.htm

Connecticut, Delaware, District of Columbia, Maine, Maryland, Massachusetts, New Hampshire, New Jersey, New York, Pennsylvania, Rhode Island, Vermont

NASA Educator Resource Center
NASA Goddard Space Flight Center
Mail Code 130.3
Greenbelt, MD 20771
tel. 301-286-8570
fax 301-286-1781
http://pao.gsfc.nasa.gov/gsfc/educ/trl/welcome.html

Eastern Shores of Virginia and Maryland

NASA Educator Resource Center
GSFC/Wallops Flight Facility
Building J-17
Wallops Island, VA 23337
tel. 757-824-2214
fax 757-824-1776
www.wff.nasa.gov/~WVC/erc.htm

Colorado, Kansas, Nebraska, New Mexico, North Dakota, Oklahoma, South Dakota, Texas

NASA Educator Resource Center
NASA Johnson Space Center
Space Center Houston
1601 NASA Road One
Houston, TX 77058
tel. 281-244-2129
fax 281-483-9638
www.spacecenter.org/educator_resource.html

Florida, Georgia, Puerto Rico, Virgin Islands

NASA Educator Resource Center
NASA Kennedy Space Center
Mail Code ERC
J. F. Kennedy Space Center, FL 32899
tel. 321-867-4090
fax 321-867-7242
http://education.ksc.nasa.gov/erc/erc.htm

Kentucky, North Carolina, South Carolina, Virginia, West Virginia

NASA Educator Resource Center
NASA Langley Research Center
Virginia Air and Space Center
600 Settlers Landing Road
Hampton, VA 23669-4033
tel. 757-727-0900 Ext. 757
fax 757-727-0898
www.vasc.org/erc

Alabama, Arkansas, Iowa, Louisiana, Missouri, Tennessee

NASA Educator Resource Center
NASA Marshall Space Flight Center
U.S. Space & Rocket Center
One Tranquility Base
Huntsville, AL 35807
tel. 256-544-5812
fax 256-544-5820
http://erc.msfc.nasa.gov

Mississippi
NASA Educator Resource Center
NASA Stennis Space Center
Building 1200
Stennis Space Center, MS 39529-6000
tel. 228-688-1974
toll-free 800-237-1821 Opt. #2
fax 228-688-3377
http://education.ssc.nasa.gov/erc/default.htm

About the Authors

Geoff Holt

Geoff Holt serves as an astronomy educator in Madison, Wisconsin. He earned his bachelor of science degree in elementary education from the University of Wisconsin–Eau Claire. He earned a master of education degree in middle grades science from the University of North Carolina at Chapel Hill (UNC–CH). He also earned a master of education degree in curriculum and instruction from National Louis University.

Mr. Holt taught middle school science in North Carolina, where his love for astronomy developed. He was a teacher leader in the original Project Earth Science team. While working on his masters degree at UNC–CH, Mr. Holt worked as an intern at the Morehead Planetarium. He currently serves as the planetarium director for the Madison Metropolitan School District in Madison, Wisconsin. Mr. Holt works with groups at the planetarium ranging from preschool to adults, develops curriculum materials, and conducts teacher workshops. He has served on the executive committee of the Great Lakes Planetarium Association for over a decade.

Mr. Holt's passion for sharing astronomy has led him to serve as an instructor for the Space Exploration Experience Project for the Blind and Visually Impaired (SEE Project), funded by a NASA Initiative to Develop Education through Astronomy and Space Science (IDEAS) grant. The IDEAS grant program provided start-up funding to explore innovative ways to integrate astronomy and space science into formal education and public outreach venues. Mr. Holt also served as an instructor for the Yerkes Astrophysics Academy for Young Scientists (YAAYS), a project at the Yerkes Observatory, funded by the National Science Foundation. He enjoys mentoring astronomy enthusiasts and future astronomers through his high school astronomy club.

Nancy W. West

Nancy West is a geoscience educator in Fort Collins, Colorado. She grew up on an island in Puget Sound, where Orion was never visible through the drizzly winter skies. She received an AB in geology from Princeton University in 1979 and an MAT from the University of North Carolina at Chapel Hill (UNC–CH) in 1991. Her studies include graduate course-work in geology and field and lab analysis of a volcanic rock from the Mojave desert.

Ms. West has taught geology at UNC–CH, chemistry and geology in Durham, North Carolina, high schools, geology for Thomas Nelson Community College, and science methods courses at Duke University and the College of William and Mary (W&M).

In addition to teaching, Ms. West has developed Earth science curricula for a middle and high school National Science Foundation project, the North Carolina Leadership Network for Earth Science Teachers. This project emphasized conducting field studies with students on campus. She has other experience with curriculum—and professional development—as the Williamsburg–James City County Public Schools' science curriculum coordinator. Recently, she has been the curriculum specialist on the Virginia Demonstration Project at W&M, a project to enhance middle school students' interest in STEM careers, using problem-based learning which features LEGO® robots.

Upon moving back to the West in 2009, Ms. West started a consulting company, Quarter Dome Consulting, LLC. When not working on projects such as Project Earth Science, she is hiking, snowshoeing, bicycling, bird-watching, reading, and enjoying her return to the West where places with wide-open dark skies abound.

Index